Survival Water Secrets

Harvesting Hidden Sources Underground

James Carleton

ISBN: 9781779665973
Imprint: Telephasic Workshop
Copyright © 2024 James Carleton.
All Rights Reserved.

Contents

Introduction   1
The Importance of Water in Survival Situations   1

Bibliography   7

Assessing Water Availability in Your Area   13
Researching Local Water Tables   13
Evaluating Surface Water Sources   20

Natural Underground Water Sources   29
Springs and Seeps   29
Underground Streams and Rivers   39
Percolation Ponds and Catchments   51

Constructing Underground Water Storage Systems   63
Building Cisterns and Wells   63
Rainwater Harvesting Systems   75

Innovative Techniques for Extracting Underground Water   87
Passive Collection Methods   87
Active Extraction Methods   97

Purifying and Storing Underground Water   109
Techniques for Water Purification   109
Long-Term Water Storage Solutions   120

Safety Considerations and Regulations   133
Understanding Water Quality and Testing   133

Bibliography 145
Permitting and Legal Considerations 145

Emergency Situations and Contingency Plans 157
Dealing with Water Scarcity and Drought 157
Natural Disasters and Other Emergencies 167

Index 181

Introduction

The Importance of Water in Survival Situations

Understanding the Human Body's Water Needs

Water is an essential component of the human body, constituting approximately 60% of an adult's body weight. This vital fluid plays a crucial role in numerous physiological processes, including temperature regulation, nutrient transport, waste elimination, and cellular function. Understanding the human body's water needs is fundamental for survival, especially in situations where access to water may be limited.

Daily Water Requirements

The amount of water an individual needs can vary significantly based on several factors, including age, gender, activity level, and environmental conditions. The National Academies of Sciences, Engineering, and Medicine recommends the following daily water intake:

- About 3.7 liters (or 13 cups) for men
- About 2.7 liters (or 9 cups) for women

These recommendations include all fluids consumed, not just water, and also account for moisture content in food. For example, fruits and vegetables can contain up to 90% water, contributing to overall hydration.

Factors Affecting Water Needs

Several factors can influence an individual's water needs:

- **Physical Activity:** Increased physical activity leads to higher water loss through sweat. Athletes or individuals engaging in strenuous activities may require additional water intake, often calculated as follows:

$$\text{Additional Water Needed (L)} = \text{Duration of Exercise (hours)} \times \text{Sweat Rate (L/hour)} \tag{1}$$

- **Climate:** Hot and humid environments increase perspiration, while high altitudes can lead to increased respiration and fluid loss. In these conditions, individuals may need to increase their water intake significantly.

- **Health Status:** Illnesses, especially those involving fever, vomiting, or diarrhea, can lead to significant fluid loss. Individuals with conditions such as diabetes or kidney disease may also have altered hydration needs.

- **Diet:** High-sodium or high-protein diets can increase water needs, as the body requires more water to metabolize these substances and excrete excess salts.

- **Age:** Older adults may have a reduced sense of thirst and may not drink enough fluids, increasing their risk of dehydration. Children, on the other hand, may need closer monitoring to ensure adequate hydration.

Consequences of Dehydration

Dehydration occurs when the body loses more fluids than it takes in. Even mild dehydration can lead to a range of symptoms, including:

- Thirst
- Dry mouth and throat
- Fatigue
- Decreased urine output
- Dizziness or lightheadedness

Severe dehydration can lead to more serious health issues, including:

- Heat injuries, such as heat exhaustion or heat stroke

- Kidney problems, including kidney stones and urinary tract infections
- Low blood volume, leading to shock

To assess hydration status, individuals can monitor urine color. Pale yellow urine typically indicates proper hydration, while dark yellow or amber urine may signal dehydration.

Hydration Strategies

To maintain adequate hydration, consider the following strategies:

- **Drink Regularly:** Establish a routine for drinking water, even if not thirsty. Carrying a water bottle can serve as a reminder to hydrate.
- **Monitor Fluid Loss:** During physical activity, weigh yourself before and after exercise to gauge fluid loss and adjust your intake accordingly.
- **Incorporate Hydrating Foods:** Include fruits and vegetables in your diet, such as cucumbers, oranges, and strawberries, which have high water content.
- **Use Electrolyte Solutions:** In cases of heavy sweating or illness, consider using electrolyte solutions to replenish lost minerals along with fluids.
- **Adjust for Environment:** In hot or dry climates, increase fluid intake to compensate for higher evaporation rates and perspiration.

In conclusion, understanding the human body's water needs is crucial for maintaining health and well-being, particularly in survival situations. By recognizing the factors that influence hydration and implementing effective strategies, individuals can ensure they meet their water requirements and avoid the detrimental effects of dehydration.

The Role of Water in Hygiene and Sanitation

Water is an essential resource not only for survival but also for maintaining hygiene and sanitation. In survival situations, the importance of water transcends mere hydration; it plays a critical role in preventing disease, promoting health, and ensuring overall well-being. This section explores the multifaceted role of water in hygiene and sanitation, the problems associated with inadequate water access, and practical examples of water use in maintaining hygiene.

The Importance of Hygiene and Sanitation

Hygiene refers to practices that promote health and prevent the spread of disease. Sanitation, on the other hand, involves the management of waste to ensure a clean and healthy environment. Water is a fundamental component of both hygiene and sanitation, as it is used for:

- **Personal Hygiene:** Water is crucial for daily activities such as bathing, washing hands, and oral hygiene. These practices reduce the risk of infections and disease transmission. For instance, handwashing with soap and water can reduce the incidence of respiratory infections by up to 23% and gastrointestinal diseases by 30% [1].

- **Food Hygiene:** Clean water is necessary for washing fruits, vegetables, and cooking utensils. Contaminated water can lead to foodborne illnesses, which are a significant cause of morbidity worldwide. The World Health Organization (WHO) estimates that approximately 2 billion people consume food irrigated with contaminated water, contributing to health risks [2].

- **Sanitation:** Water is vital for flushing toilets and managing sewage systems. Proper sanitation prevents the contamination of water sources and reduces the risk of waterborne diseases. According to the WHO, inadequate sanitation is linked to the spread of diseases such as cholera, dysentery, and typhoid fever [3].

Problems Associated with Inadequate Water Access

The lack of access to clean water can lead to severe hygiene and sanitation challenges. Some of the primary problems include:

- **Increased Disease Transmission:** Inadequate water for personal hygiene and sanitation can result in higher rates of infectious diseases. For example, during the 2010 cholera outbreak in Haiti, the spread of the disease was exacerbated by a lack of clean water and sanitation facilities [4].

- **Environmental Contamination:** Without proper sanitation, human waste can contaminate local water sources, leading to a cycle of disease transmission. This is particularly problematic in areas with high population density and inadequate waste management systems.

- **Social and Economic Impact:** The burden of water-related diseases can strain healthcare systems and reduce productivity. Families may spend significant time and resources seeking medical treatment, which can hinder economic development.

Practical Examples of Water Use in Hygiene and Sanitation

To illustrate the role of water in hygiene and sanitation, consider the following practical examples:

1. **Handwashing Stations:** In emergency situations, setting up handwashing stations with clean water and soap is critical. These stations can be established in refugee camps, disaster relief areas, or temporary shelters to promote hand hygiene and reduce disease transmission.

2. **Water Purification Techniques:** In survival scenarios, individuals can employ various water purification methods to ensure safe drinking water. Techniques such as boiling, using water purification tablets, or solar disinfection (SODIS) can make contaminated water safe for consumption, thus supporting both personal hygiene and sanitation efforts.

3. **Composting Toilets:** In areas with limited water access, composting toilets can be an effective solution for sanitation. These toilets use minimal water and convert human waste into compost, reducing environmental contamination and promoting hygiene.

Conclusion

In conclusion, water is indispensable for hygiene and sanitation, playing a crucial role in preventing disease and promoting health. The challenges posed by inadequate water access can lead to severe public health issues, emphasizing the need for sustainable water management practices. By understanding the importance of water in hygiene and sanitation, individuals can take actionable steps to improve their health and well-being, particularly in survival situations.

Bibliography

[1] World Health Organization. (2020). Hand hygiene. Retrieved from https://www.who.int/news-room/fact-sheets/detail/hand-hygiene

[2] World Health Organization. (2015). Foodborne diseases. Retrieved from https://www.who.int/news-room/fact-sheets/detail/foodborne-illn

[3] World Health Organization. (2019). Sanitation. Retrieved from https://www.who.int/news-room/fact-sheets/detail/sanitation

[4] World Health Organization. (2011). Cholera in Haiti: A public health crisis. Retrieved from https://www.who.int/haiti/cholera

Common Survival Water Sources

In survival situations, access to water is paramount. Understanding the various sources of water available in the environment can significantly enhance your chances of survival. This section explores common survival water sources, their characteristics, and the challenges associated with each.

Surface Water Sources

Surface water is the most visible and often the most accessible source of water. It includes rivers, lakes, ponds, and streams. While surface water is abundant in many areas, it comes with several considerations:

- **Quality Concerns:** Surface water can be contaminated with pollutants, pathogens, and sediments. It is essential to assess the clarity and odor of the water before consumption. Turbid water, for instance, may harbor harmful microorganisms.

- **Seasonal Variability:** The availability of surface water can fluctuate significantly with the seasons. During dry periods, lakes and streams may dry up, necessitating alternative sources.

- **Accessibility:** The physical location of surface water sources can impact their accessibility. Steep banks, dense vegetation, or remote locations may hinder access to these water supplies.

Groundwater Sources

Groundwater is another vital source of water, found beneath the Earth's surface. It can be accessed through wells, springs, and seepage. Groundwater typically offers higher quality water than surface sources, but it requires specific techniques to locate and extract.

- **Wells:** Wells can be dug or drilled to access groundwater. The depth of the water table varies based on geographical location and seasonal changes. The formula for estimating the depth of the water table is:

$$D = H - h \qquad (2)$$

  where D is the depth of the water table, H is the height of the land surface, and h is the height of the water in the well.

- **Springs:** Springs occur when groundwater naturally flows to the surface, often forming small streams. Identifying springs can be beneficial, as they typically provide clean, fresh water. Look for signs such as wet ground, vegetation, or animal tracks leading to a water source.

- **Seepage:** In some areas, water may seep out of the ground, creating small puddles or wet areas. These seeps can be valuable sources of water, especially in arid environments.

Rainwater Harvesting

Rainwater harvesting involves collecting and storing rainwater for future use. This method can be particularly effective in regions with seasonal rainfall. Key considerations include:

- **Collection Systems:** To harvest rainwater, you can use roofs, gutters, and storage tanks. The efficiency of your collection system can be estimated using the following equation:

$$V = A \times R \times C \tag{3}$$

where V is the volume of water collected, A is the area of the collection surface (e.g., roof), R is the rainfall depth, and C is the runoff coefficient (a factor that accounts for losses due to evaporation and absorption).

- **Storage Solutions:** Proper storage of harvested rainwater is crucial to prevent contamination and ensure long-term usability. Containers should be opaque to limit algae growth and should be regularly cleaned to maintain water quality.

Atmospheric Water Generation

In areas with high humidity, atmospheric water can be harvested using various techniques, such as dew collection or fog nets. These methods capitalize on the natural condensation of moisture in the air.

- **Dew Collection:** Dew forms on surfaces during cool nights. To collect dew, place a clean, non-absorbent surface (like plastic sheeting) in a location where dew is likely to form. The collected dew can then be gathered and stored.

- **Fog Nets:** In fog-prone areas, specially designed nets can capture water droplets from fog. As fog passes through the net, droplets coalesce and drip into collection containers.

Desalination

In coastal regions, seawater can be converted to freshwater through desalination processes. While this method is energy-intensive, it can be a crucial survival strategy in extreme situations.

- **Solar Desalination:** A simple method involves using solar energy to heat seawater, causing evaporation. The vapor can then be condensed into freshwater. This process can be modeled by the following equation:

$$Q = m \cdot L \tag{4}$$

where Q is the heat required for evaporation, m is the mass of the water, and L is the latent heat of vaporization.

- **Reverse Osmosis:** This method uses a membrane to separate salt from water. While effective, it requires a pressure source and is more complex than solar desalination.

Conclusion

Each of these common survival water sources has its unique advantages and challenges. Understanding these sources and their characteristics can empower individuals to make informed decisions in survival situations. Proper knowledge and preparation can mean the difference between life and death when access to clean water is critical.

The Benefits of Harvesting Hidden Sources Underground

In survival situations, access to clean and reliable water is paramount. While surface water sources such as rivers, lakes, and ponds are often the first to be considered, they can be unreliable due to seasonal changes, pollution, and evaporation. In contrast, hidden underground water sources offer several distinct advantages that can be crucial for survival.

Reliability and Consistency

One of the primary benefits of harvesting hidden sources underground is their reliability. Underground aquifers and springs often maintain a more consistent supply of water than surface sources. For instance, aquifers can store vast amounts of water, which is replenished through rainfall and surface runoff. This can be particularly advantageous in arid climates where surface water may dry up during prolonged droughts.

$$\text{Water Table Height} = \text{Recharge Rate} - \text{Discharge Rate} \quad (5)$$

This equation illustrates that the height of the water table (the upper surface of groundwater) is influenced by the balance between the recharge (from precipitation and infiltration) and discharge (to springs, wells, or evaporation). A well-managed aquifer can provide a sustainable water supply, making it a vital resource in survival situations.

Protection from Contamination

Underground water sources are generally less susceptible to contamination compared to surface water. Surface water is exposed to pollutants from agricultural runoff, industrial discharges, and urban waste. In contrast, water that seeps through soil layers is naturally filtered, which can significantly reduce the presence of harmful pathogens and chemicals.

For example, a study conducted by the United States Geological Survey (USGS) found that groundwater typically has lower concentrations of nitrate and other contaminants compared to surface water bodies. The natural filtration process that occurs as water percolates through soil and rock layers can enhance the quality of the water harvested from underground sources.

Temperature Regulation

Another benefit of harvesting underground water is its temperature stability. Water stored underground is generally cooler than surface water, which can be advantageous in hot climates. Cooler water is not only more pleasant to drink but can also help in preserving food and other perishable items.

The temperature of groundwater can be approximated using the following equation:

$$T_g = T_s - (d \cdot k) \qquad (6)$$

Where: - T_g is the temperature of the groundwater, - T_s is the surface temperature, - d is the depth of the water source, - k is the thermal gradient (typically around 25-30 °C/km).

This equation indicates that as depth increases, the groundwater temperature stabilizes, providing a cooler alternative to surface water.

Accessibility in Diverse Climates

Hidden water sources can be crucial in diverse climatic conditions. In areas prone to extreme weather, such as heavy rainfall or drought, underground sources can provide a reliable water supply when surface sources are compromised. For instance, during a drought, access to groundwater through wells can be a lifesaver, while surface water may become scarce.

In contrast, during heavy rains, surface water bodies can become contaminated with runoff, making underground sources a safer alternative. The ability to tap into these hidden resources can significantly enhance survival odds in fluctuating environmental conditions.

Long-term Water Security

By investing in the harvesting of underground water sources, individuals and communities can secure long-term access to water. Building systems such as cisterns, wells, and percolation ponds can create a sustainable water supply that is less affected by the immediate environmental conditions.

For example, constructing a cistern to collect rainwater and store it underground can provide a buffer against seasonal variations in water availability. This practice not only ensures a consistent water supply but also promotes water conservation and management.

Cost-Effectiveness

Harvesting underground water can also be more cost-effective in the long run. While the initial investment in drilling wells or constructing cisterns may be significant, the ongoing costs associated with maintaining these systems are often lower than those of relying on surface water sources.

Additionally, underground water systems require less infrastructure and maintenance than extensive surface water systems, which may need regular cleaning, dredging, and management to prevent contamination and ensure accessibility.

Conclusion

In summary, the benefits of harvesting hidden sources underground are manifold, offering reliability, protection from contamination, temperature regulation, accessibility across diverse climates, long-term water security, and cost-effectiveness. As individuals and communities prepare for potential survival situations, understanding and utilizing these underground water sources can significantly enhance their resilience and ability to thrive in challenging conditions. By leveraging these hidden resources, one can ensure a sustainable and safe water supply, which is essential for survival.

Assessing Water Availability in Your Area

Researching Local Water Tables

Locating Reliable Sources of Information

In order to effectively assess water availability in your area, it is crucial to locate reliable sources of information regarding local water tables. Understanding the depth, quality, and dynamics of groundwater resources can significantly enhance your ability to harvest hidden sources underground. This section will outline various strategies for finding trustworthy data, including government resources, academic studies, and local expertise.

Government Resources

One of the most reliable sources of information regarding water tables is government agencies. Many countries have dedicated geological surveys or environmental agencies that monitor and publish data on groundwater levels and quality. In the United States, for example, the United States Geological Survey (USGS) provides extensive data through its National Water Information System (NWIS). This system includes real-time data on streamflow, groundwater levels, and water quality across the nation.

$$\text{Groundwater Level} = \text{Surface Elevation} - \text{Depth to Water Table} \qquad (7)$$

This equation illustrates how to determine the groundwater level by subtracting the depth to the water table from the surface elevation. By accessing government databases, you can obtain both historical and current data on groundwater levels, which can be instrumental in evaluating the viability of harvesting underground water.

Academic Studies

Academic institutions often conduct research on local hydrology and geology, providing valuable insights into groundwater resources. University libraries and online academic databases such as Google Scholar or JSTOR can be excellent places to find peer-reviewed articles and theses related to groundwater studies in your area. These studies often include detailed analyses of water tables, aquifer characteristics, and the impacts of various environmental factors on water availability.

For instance, a study conducted by Smith et al. (2020) on the aquifer recharge rates in the Midwest found that land use significantly affects groundwater levels. Their research indicated that agricultural practices can lead to a decline in water table levels, emphasizing the importance of understanding local land use when assessing water availability.

Local Experts

Consulting local experts can also provide invaluable information on water tables. Hydrogeologists, environmental consultants, and local water management authorities possess practical knowledge that may not be available in published studies or government reports. Engaging with these professionals can help you understand the nuances of the local water system, including seasonal variations and the impact of climate change on groundwater resources.

When seeking local expertise, consider the following approaches:

- **Attend Community Meetings:** Local government or environmental organizations often hold public meetings to discuss water management issues. These gatherings can be an excellent opportunity to ask questions and gather insights from experts.

- **Networking:** Building relationships with local farmers, landowners, and residents can also provide anecdotal evidence about water availability and historical trends in your area.

- **Consulting Local Universities:** Many universities have extension programs that connect researchers with the community. These programs can provide access to experts who can offer tailored advice based on local conditions.

Analyzing Geological Surveys

Geological surveys are another critical resource for understanding local water tables. These surveys often include maps and reports that detail the geological formations in an area, including aquifers, which are underground layers of water-bearing rock. Understanding the geology is essential for predicting where groundwater might be found and how it can be accessed.

For example, a geological survey might reveal the presence of a limestone aquifer, which is known for its ability to store and transmit water effectively. Knowing the type of geological formation present in your area can guide your efforts in locating underground water sources.

$$\text{Hydraulic Conductivity (K)} = \frac{Q}{A \cdot \Delta h / L} \tag{8}$$

In this equation, Q is the discharge (volume of water per unit time), A is the cross-sectional area through which the water flows, Δh is the change in hydraulic head, and L is the length of the flow path. Understanding hydraulic conductivity helps in assessing the potential yield of a groundwater source.

Conclusion

In conclusion, locating reliable sources of information about local water tables is essential for effective water harvesting. By utilizing government resources, academic studies, local expertise, and geological surveys, you can gain a comprehensive understanding of groundwater availability in your area. This knowledge will not only aid in immediate survival situations but also contribute to long-term water management strategies.

Consulting Local Experts for Water Table Data

When it comes to understanding the water table in your area, consulting local experts is an invaluable step. These professionals, including hydrogeologists, environmental scientists, and local water management authorities, possess specialized knowledge and resources that can significantly enhance your understanding of groundwater availability and quality. This section will cover the importance of engaging with local experts, the types of information they can provide, and effective strategies for consultation.

Importance of Local Expertise

Local experts have a deep understanding of the regional geology, hydrology, and historical water usage patterns. They can provide insights into:

- **Geological Variability:** The subsurface geology can vary widely even within small areas. Local experts can explain how different rock formations affect groundwater movement and storage.

- **Historical Data:** Experts often have access to historical water table data, which can reveal trends over time, such as seasonal fluctuations and long-term changes due to climate or human activity.

- **Regulatory Framework:** Knowledge of local regulations regarding water rights and extraction is crucial. Experts can guide you through the legal landscape, helping you understand what is permissible in your area.

Types of Information Provided by Experts

Engaging with local experts can yield a wealth of information, including:

- **Water Table Depth and Fluctuations:** Experts can provide current data on the depth of the water table and how it varies seasonally or in response to rainfall.

- **Quality of Groundwater:** Understanding the chemical composition and potential contaminants in local groundwater is essential. Experts can conduct tests and interpret results, providing clarity on water safety.

- **Sustainable Practices:** Local experts can offer advice on sustainable water extraction methods that minimize environmental impact and ensure long-term water availability.

Strategies for Effective Consultation

To make the most of your consultation with local experts, consider the following strategies:

1. **Prepare Specific Questions:** Before meeting with an expert, prepare a list of questions tailored to your needs. This could include inquiries about water table depth, quality testing methods, or recommendations for sustainable practices.

2. **Utilize Local Resources:** Many regions have local universities, research institutions, or government agencies focused on water resources. Reach out to these organizations to find experts who can assist you.

3. **Attend Workshops and Seminars:** Local environmental groups or universities often host workshops on water management. Participating in these events can provide valuable networking opportunities and further knowledge.

4. **Follow Up:** After your initial consultation, maintain communication. Experts can provide ongoing support and updates on new developments or changes in local water regulations.

Examples of Local Expertise Utilization

To illustrate the benefits of consulting local experts, consider the following examples:

- **Case Study 1: Rural Community Water Management**
  In a rural community facing declining water levels, local hydrogeologists conducted a study on the groundwater recharge rates. They discovered that certain agricultural practices were depleting the aquifer faster than it could recharge. The community implemented new irrigation techniques based on the expert's recommendations, resulting in a sustainable balance between water usage and aquifer replenishment.

- **Case Study 2: Urban Development Planning**
  An urban planning department consulted with environmental scientists to assess the impact of a new housing development on local water resources. The experts provided data on the existing water table and its fluctuations, enabling planners to design the project while minimizing impacts on groundwater. They also recommended specific landscaping techniques that would enhance rainwater infiltration, further protecting local water resources.

Conclusion

Consulting local experts for water table data is a critical step in effectively managing and utilizing underground water resources. Their specialized knowledge and access to relevant data can help you make informed decisions about water sourcing, usage, and sustainability. By preparing adequately for consultations and engaging with the right professionals, you can enhance your understanding of local water dynamics and contribute to responsible water management practices in your area.

Analyzing Geological Surveys to Determine Water Availability

Geological surveys are essential tools for assessing water availability in a given area. These surveys provide detailed information about the geological and hydrological characteristics of the terrain, which can significantly influence water accessibility and quality. Understanding how to analyze these surveys allows individuals to make informed decisions regarding water sourcing for survival situations.

Understanding Geological Surveys

A geological survey typically includes various data types, such as topographic maps, soil composition, rock formations, and groundwater levels. The primary goal is to identify the distribution and movement of groundwater, which is crucial for locating potential water sources.

$$\text{Hydraulic Conductivity}(K) = \frac{Q}{A \cdot \Delta h / L} \qquad (9)$$

Where: - Q is the discharge (volume per time), - A is the cross-sectional area, - Δh is the change in hydraulic head, - L is the length over which the head change occurs.

The hydraulic conductivity K indicates how easily water can flow through the geological materials, which is vital for understanding potential water availability.

Types of Geological Surveys

1. **Topographic Maps**: These maps illustrate the elevation and contour of the land, helping to identify potential areas for water accumulation, such as valleys and depressions where groundwater may surface.
2. **Soil Surveys**: Soil characteristics affect water retention and infiltration rates. Clay soils, for example, have low permeability, while sandy soils allow for rapid drainage. Analyzing soil types helps in determining how much water can be stored in the ground.
3. **Geological Cross-Sections**: These diagrams represent the subsurface geology, showing the arrangement of different rock layers. They can reveal the presence of aquifers, which are crucial for sustainable water sourcing.

Analyzing Groundwater Levels

Groundwater level data from surveys can indicate the depth at which water can be found. Monitoring groundwater levels over time can reveal trends such as seasonal fluctuations, which are critical for planning water extraction.

$$\text{Hydraulic Gradient}(i) = \frac{\Delta h}{L} \qquad (10)$$

Where: - Δh is the difference in hydraulic head between two points, - L is the distance between those points.

The hydraulic gradient helps to understand the flow direction of groundwater, which can be essential for locating wells or other extraction points.

Case Study: Analyzing a Geological Survey for Water Sourcing

Consider a hypothetical scenario in a semi-arid region where a survivalist seeks to find water. By analyzing the geological survey data, they discover the following:

- The topographic map reveals a low-lying area that collects runoff from surrounding hills. - Soil surveys indicate a clay layer beneath the surface, suggesting good water retention capabilities. - Geological cross-sections show a shallow aquifer located approximately 15 meters below the surface.

Based on this analysis, the survivalist can:

- Dig a well in the low-lying area to access the aquifer. - Utilize the clay layer to create a percolation pond that captures rainwater runoff. - Monitor groundwater levels to ensure sustainable extraction rates.

Challenges in Analyzing Geological Surveys

While geological surveys provide valuable insights, challenges may arise:

- **Data Availability**: In some regions, geological data may be sparse or outdated, making it difficult to assess current water availability accurately.

- **Interpreting Complex Geologies**: Areas with complex geological formations may require advanced knowledge to interpret correctly, necessitating consultation with geologists or hydrologists.

- **Environmental Changes**: Natural disasters, climate change, and human activities can alter geological features, impacting water availability. Continuous monitoring and re-evaluation of geological surveys are necessary to adapt to these changes.

Conclusion

Analyzing geological surveys is a critical step in determining water availability. By understanding the various components of these surveys, individuals can better assess potential water sources, implement effective harvesting strategies, and ensure sustainable water use in survival situations. As water scarcity becomes an increasingly pressing issue, the ability to navigate and interpret geological data will be an invaluable skill in the quest for reliable water supplies.

Evaluating Surface Water Sources

Recognizing the Limitations of Surface Water

Surface water, which includes rivers, lakes, ponds, and streams, is often the most accessible source of water for survival situations. However, it comes with a set of limitations and challenges that can significantly impact its reliability and safety for human consumption. Understanding these limitations is crucial for anyone relying on surface water during emergencies or survival scenarios.

Variability in Availability

One of the primary limitations of surface water is its variability in availability. Seasonal changes, climate conditions, and geographical factors can lead to fluctuations in water levels. For instance, during dry seasons or prolonged droughts, rivers and lakes may experience significant reductions in water volume. This can make it difficult to find sufficient quantities of water when needed.

$$\text{Water Availability} = f(\text{Precipitation, Evapotranspiration, Infiltration}) \quad (11)$$

Where: - f is a function representing the relationship between various factors affecting water availability. - Precipitation is the amount of rainfall in a given period. - Evapotranspiration is the loss of water due to evaporation and transpiration from plants. - Infiltration refers to the process by which water enters the soil.

Contamination Risks

Surface water is susceptible to contamination from various sources, including agricultural runoff, industrial discharges, and urban pollution. Contaminants can include pathogens, heavy metals, and chemicals that pose serious health risks. For example, E. coli bacteria from livestock waste can contaminate nearby water sources, making them unsafe for consumption.

$$\text{Contamination Risk} = \frac{\text{Concentration of Contaminants}}{\text{Water Volume}} \quad (12)$$

This equation illustrates that higher concentrations of contaminants in a given volume of water increase the overall contamination risk. Regular testing and monitoring of surface water sources are essential to assess their safety.

Quality Variability

The quality of surface water can vary significantly, even within the same water body. Factors such as sediment load, temperature, and biological activity can affect water quality. For instance, during heavy rainfall, runoff can introduce sediments and pollutants into lakes and rivers, leading to turbid water that may not be suitable for drinking without proper treatment.

$$\text{Water Quality Index} = \frac{(\text{Physical} + \text{Chemical} + \text{Biological})}{3} \quad (13)$$

Where: - Physical refers to turbidity and temperature. - Chemical includes pH, dissolved oxygen, and contaminant levels. - Biological assesses the presence of pathogens and microorganisms.

Accessibility Challenges

In some cases, surface water sources may not be easily accessible. Factors such as geographical barriers, private land ownership, or environmental regulations can hinder access to water bodies. For instance, a river may be located in a remote area that requires significant effort to reach, or it may flow through private property, necessitating permission for access.

Seasonal Changes and Ice Cover

In colder climates, surface water can be affected by seasonal changes, particularly freezing during winter months. Ice cover can prevent access to water and complicate extraction methods. Even in milder climates, seasonal variations can lead to changes in water quality and quantity, further complicating the reliability of surface water sources.

Competition for Resources

In many regions, surface water is a shared resource, leading to competition among users. This can result in conflicts over water rights, especially in areas experiencing drought or increased demand. For example, farmers, municipalities, and industries may all vie for access to the same river, leading to potential shortages for individual users.

Ecological Impact

Finally, reliance on surface water can have ecological consequences. Over-extraction of water from rivers and lakes can disrupt local ecosystems, harming fish populations and other aquatic life. Sustainable water management practices are essential to ensure that surface water use does not lead to long-term ecological damage.

Conclusion

While surface water can provide immediate access to water resources, it is essential to recognize its limitations. Variability in availability, contamination risks, quality fluctuations, accessibility challenges, seasonal changes, competition for resources, and ecological impacts all pose significant challenges. Understanding these limitations allows individuals to develop more robust water sourcing strategies, including the exploration of underground water sources and the implementation of effective purification methods.

Identifying Nearby Rivers, Lakes, and Ponds

In survival situations, recognizing and utilizing nearby surface water sources such as rivers, lakes, and ponds can be crucial for sustaining life. These bodies of water not only provide hydration but can also be used for hygiene and sanitation. This section will delve into the methods for identifying these water sources, their significance, and the challenges associated with their use.

Understanding the Importance of Surface Water

Surface water sources are often the most accessible forms of water in a given environment. Rivers, lakes, and ponds can serve as immediate solutions for hydration and other survival needs. However, the availability and quality of these water sources can vary significantly based on geographical and climatic conditions.

Methods for Identifying Surface Water Sources

To effectively locate rivers, lakes, and ponds in your vicinity, consider the following methods:

1. **Topographic Maps:** Utilize topographic maps to identify the contours of the land. Rivers and lakes are often depicted as blue lines and areas, respectively. These maps can provide insights into the elevation changes that indicate the presence of water bodies.

2. **Satellite Imagery:** Modern technology allows for the use of satellite imagery to locate large bodies of water. Online services such as Google Earth can be particularly useful for visualizing the landscape and identifying potential water sources.

3. **Local Knowledge:** Engaging with local residents or experts can yield valuable information about hidden water sources. Local knowledge often includes insights about seasonal changes in water availability and the quality of various water bodies.

4. **Wildlife Observation:** Animals often congregate near water sources. Observing the movement patterns of wildlife, particularly birds and mammals, can lead you to rivers, lakes, or ponds.

Evaluating the Quality and Accessibility of Surface Water

Once potential water sources have been identified, it is crucial to evaluate their quality and accessibility. This involves:

1. **Accessibility:** Assess how easy it is to reach the water source. Consider factors such as terrain, vegetation density, and proximity to your location. Ensure that the route to the water source is safe and does not expose you to potential hazards.

2. **Water Quality Assessment:** Surface water can be contaminated by pollutants, pathogens, and sediments. Before consuming water from these sources, it is essential to conduct a preliminary assessment of its quality. Look for clear water free of visible debris and avoid sources near industrial areas or agricultural runoff.

3. **Water Testing:** If possible, utilize portable water testing kits to analyze the water for contaminants such as bacteria, nitrates, and heavy metals. This step is vital for ensuring the water is safe for consumption.

Common Problems Associated with Surface Water Sources

While rivers, lakes, and ponds can provide essential water, several challenges may arise:

- **Seasonal Variability:** The availability of surface water can fluctuate with the seasons. During droughts, rivers may dry up, and lakes may shrink, making it essential to plan for such variations.

- **Contamination Risks:** Surface water is susceptible to contamination from natural and anthropogenic sources. Flooding can introduce pollutants, while runoff can carry fertilizers and pesticides into water bodies.

- **Competition for Resources:** In survival situations, other individuals or wildlife may also depend on the same water sources, leading to competition for this vital resource. It is essential to be aware of your surroundings and the potential for conflicts over water access.

Examples of Surface Water Sources

To illustrate the concepts discussed, consider the following examples:

- **Rivers:** The Colorado River in the United States is a significant water source that flows through various terrains, providing water for millions. However, its flow can be affected by seasonal snowmelt and drought conditions.

- **Lakes:** Lake Baikal in Russia is the world's deepest and oldest freshwater lake. Despite its size, access to clean water can be a challenge due to pollution from nearby settlements.

- **Ponds:** Small ponds can often be found in rural areas and forests. While they may provide a quick water source, they are more prone to contamination and should be treated with caution.

In conclusion, identifying and evaluating nearby rivers, lakes, and ponds is a critical skill for survival. By employing various methods to locate these water sources and understanding the challenges associated with their use, individuals can better prepare for situations where water scarcity may arise. Always prioritize safety and water quality when relying on surface water for hydration and other needs.

Assessing the Quality and Accessibility of Surface Water

In survival situations, surface water sources such as rivers, lakes, and ponds can provide essential hydration. However, not all surface water is suitable for consumption. This section delves into the methods for assessing the quality and accessibility of these vital resources, ensuring that you can make informed decisions when water scarcity looms.

Understanding Water Quality

Water quality is determined by various physical, chemical, and biological parameters. Assessing these parameters is crucial for ensuring the safety of surface water sources. The following key factors should be evaluated:

- **Physical Characteristics:** Clarity, color, and temperature can indicate the presence of contaminants. Turbidity, measured in Nephelometric Turbidity Units (NTU), is a common indicator of suspended particles. Clean drinking water typically has a turbidity of less than 1 NTU.

- **Chemical Composition:** The presence of pollutants, such as heavy metals (lead, mercury) and nutrients (nitrates, phosphates), can severely impact water quality. Chemical tests can quantify these contaminants. For example, the concentration of nitrates can be measured using the equation:

$$\text{Nitrate concentration (mg/L)} = \frac{\text{Volume of nitrate solution (mL)} \times \text{Nitrate concent}}{\text{Total volume of water sample (mL)}}$$
(14)

- **Biological Indicators:** The presence of pathogens, such as bacteria and viruses, is a critical concern. Common indicators include Escherichia coli (E. coli) and coliform bacteria. A higher concentration of these organisms indicates a higher risk of waterborne diseases.

Accessibility Considerations

Accessibility to surface water is as important as its quality. Assessing accessibility involves evaluating the physical characteristics of the water source and the surrounding environment.

- **Proximity:** The distance to the water source affects your ability to retrieve it. Ideally, a water source should be within a short walking distance to minimize energy expenditure. Consider using the following formula to estimate the time required to reach a water source:

$$\text{Time (hours)} = \frac{\text{Distance (km)}}{\text{Walking speed (km/h)}} \qquad (15)$$

For example, if a water source is 2 km away and your walking speed is 5 km/h, it will take approximately 0.4 hours (or 24 minutes) to reach it.

- **Terrain:** The nature of the terrain can significantly affect accessibility. Steep, rocky, or marshy areas may hinder access. Evaluate the landscape and plan your route accordingly to avoid unnecessary obstacles.

- **Seasonal Variability:** Surface water availability can fluctuate based on seasonal changes. For instance, rivers may dry up during droughts or become flooded during heavy rains. Understanding local climate patterns and seasonal variations can help predict water availability.

- **Legal and Environmental Considerations:** Access to surface water may be restricted by legal regulations or environmental protections. Familiarize yourself with local laws regarding water usage, especially in protected areas. Additionally, consider the environmental impact of accessing water sources, as over-extraction can harm ecosystems.

Practical Assessment Techniques

To effectively assess the quality and accessibility of surface water, various practical techniques can be employed:

- **Field Testing Kits:** Portable water testing kits allow for on-site assessment of water quality parameters such as pH, turbidity, and the presence of bacteria. These kits provide immediate feedback, enabling quick decision-making.

- **Visual Inspection:** A thorough visual inspection can reveal a lot about water quality. Look for signs of pollution, such as floating debris, discoloration, or unusual odors. Avoid water sources that appear contaminated or have a foul smell.

- **Sampling:** Collect water samples from different locations within the same water body to assess variability in quality. Use clean containers to avoid contamination during sampling. Label samples with the date, time, and location for future reference.

- **Local Knowledge:** Consulting local residents or experts can provide valuable insights into the quality and accessibility of surface water sources. They may have historical knowledge of water conditions and seasonal changes that can inform your assessment.

Conclusion

Assessing the quality and accessibility of surface water is a critical skill in survival situations. By understanding the physical, chemical, and biological characteristics of water, as well as evaluating accessibility, you can make informed decisions about which sources to use. Employing practical assessment techniques will further enhance your ability to secure safe drinking water, ensuring your health and survival in challenging conditions. Always prioritize water quality and be aware of the legal and environmental implications of your water sourcing strategies.

Natural Underground Water Sources

Springs and Seeps

Identifying Springs in Your Area

Identifying springs in your area is a crucial step in securing a reliable water source for survival situations. Springs are natural outlets where groundwater flows to the surface, and they can provide a consistent and often clean water supply. Understanding how to locate these springs can enhance your preparedness and resilience in times of need.

Understanding Springs

Springs occur when the water table intersects the land surface, allowing groundwater to flow out. The flow of water from springs can be influenced by geological formations, rainfall patterns, and the seasonal variation of the water table.

Mathematically, the flow rate of a spring can be described by the following equation:

$$Q = A \cdot v \tag{16}$$

where:

- Q is the discharge (flow rate) in cubic meters per second (m³/s),
- A is the cross-sectional area of the spring's outlet in square meters (m²), and
- v is the velocity of water flow in meters per second (m/s).

To locate springs effectively, you need to understand the local geology and hydrology. Springs are often found in areas with specific geological features such as limestone, sandstone, or volcanic rock, which can facilitate the movement of groundwater.

Techniques for Identifying Springs

1. Topographic Maps   Utilizing topographic maps is one of the most effective methods for locating springs. Look for contour lines that indicate changes in elevation. Springs are often found at the base of hills or slopes where the land flattens out. The presence of contour lines converging can indicate a potential spring location.

2. Vegetation Indicators   Certain types of vegetation can signal the presence of a spring. Look for lush, green areas or clusters of specific plants, such as willows or ferns, which thrive in moist conditions. These plants often indicate a consistent water source nearby.

3. Soil Moisture Analysis   Conducting soil moisture analysis can provide insights into potential spring locations. Areas with consistently high moisture levels, especially during dry periods, may suggest the presence of groundwater emerging at the surface. Use a soil moisture meter or conduct a simple hand test by digging a small hole and observing the soil's dampness.

4. Local Knowledge and Resources   Consulting local experts, such as geologists, hydrologists, or seasoned survivalists, can be invaluable. They may provide insights into historical spring locations or share knowledge about seasonal variations in spring flow. Additionally, local government agencies or universities may have geological surveys and hydrology studies that can help identify springs in your area.

Practical Examples

Consider a scenario in a mountainous region where you are seeking a water source. By analyzing topographic maps, you identify a series of contour lines that indicate a slope. Upon visiting the area, you observe a vibrant patch of vegetation at the foot of the slope. A closer inspection reveals a small stream trickling from the ground, confirming the presence of a spring.

In contrast, in a flat, arid region, springs may be more challenging to locate. However, by monitoring soil moisture and engaging with local residents, you

SPRINGS AND SEEPS

discover that a nearby dry creek bed often flows after heavy rains, indicating a potential spring upstream.

Challenges in Identifying Springs

While identifying springs can be rewarding, it also presents challenges. Seasonal variations can affect visibility, and springs may dry up during prolonged droughts. Moreover, some springs may be contaminated due to proximity to human activities or agricultural runoff. It is essential to conduct thorough assessments of water quality before relying on any spring as a water source.

In conclusion, identifying springs in your area requires a combination of geological knowledge, observational skills, and local insights. By employing various techniques and understanding the environmental context, you can effectively locate springs and secure a vital water source for survival situations. Always remember to assess the quality of the water from these springs before consumption to ensure your safety and health.

Assessing the Flow and Reliability of Springs

Assessing the flow and reliability of springs is crucial for determining their suitability as a water source in survival situations. Springs are natural outlets where groundwater emerges at the surface, and their flow can vary significantly based on several factors, including geological conditions, seasonal changes, and human activity. This section will explore the methods for assessing the flow rate of springs, understanding their reliability, and evaluating the factors that influence their water output.

Understanding Spring Flow

The flow of a spring is generally measured in terms of discharge, which is the volume of water that flows from the spring per unit time. Discharge can be quantified using the following equation:

$$Q = A \cdot v \tag{17}$$

where:

- Q = discharge (m³/s)

- A = cross-sectional area of the flow (m²)

- v = velocity of the water (m/s)

To accurately assess the discharge of a spring, you can use the following steps:

1. **Identify the Spring Source**: Locate the spring and determine the area from which the water is emerging. This may involve observing the flow and surrounding topography.

2. **Measure the Cross-Sectional Area**: Using a measuring tape, determine the width and depth of the flow. The cross-sectional area can be calculated as:

$$A = w \cdot d \tag{18}$$

where w is the width of the flow and d is the depth.

3. **Measure the Flow Velocity**: The velocity can be measured using a float method, where a small object is released upstream and the time it takes to travel a known distance downstream is recorded. The velocity can be calculated as:

$$v = \frac{d}{t} \tag{19}$$

where d is the distance traveled (m) and t is the time taken (s).

4. **Calculate Discharge**: Substitute the values of A and v into Equation (1) to find the discharge rate of the spring.

Factors Affecting Spring Flow

Several factors can influence the flow and reliability of springs:

- **Geological Conditions**: The type of rock and soil in the area can affect the permeability and the amount of water that can be stored underground. For example, limestone formations often yield more water due to their ability to dissolve and create cavities that can store groundwater.

- **Seasonal Variations**: Spring flow can vary with the seasons. During wet seasons, springs may flow abundantly, while in dry seasons, flow may diminish significantly. Long-term monitoring of flow rates can help understand these seasonal patterns.

- **Human Activities**: Activities such as construction, agriculture, and water extraction can impact the natural flow of springs. It is important to assess any nearby human activities that could affect water availability.

- **Hydrological Cycle**: The overall hydrological cycle, including precipitation, evaporation, and groundwater recharge, plays a significant role in the reliability of springs. Understanding local weather patterns can provide insights into expected changes in spring flow.

Monitoring Spring Reliability

To ensure a spring is a reliable water source, it is important to monitor its flow over time. Here are some recommended practices:

1. **Regular Measurements**: Conduct regular measurements of discharge, especially during different seasons, to establish a flow profile for the spring.

2. **Water Quality Testing**: Regularly test the water quality to ensure it remains safe for consumption. Contaminants can vary with flow changes, so consistent testing is essential.

3. **Observation of Changes**: Keep an eye on any changes in the surrounding environment that may affect the spring, such as increased development or changes in land use.

Example Case Study

Consider a spring located in a limestone region, which has shown a consistent flow of approximately 0.05 m³/s during the wet season and drops to 0.01 m³/s during the dry season. By measuring the flow at different times, the following data was collected:

- Wet Season:
    - Width (w) = 1.5 m
    - Depth (d) = 0.2 m
    - Flow Velocity (v) = 0.25 m/s

- Dry Season:
    - Width (w) = 0.8 m
    - Depth (d) = 0.1 m
    - Flow Velocity (v) = 0.15 m/s

Calculating the discharge for the wet season:

$$A = w \cdot d = 1.5\,\text{m} \cdot 0.2\,\text{m} = 0.3\,\text{m}^2$$
$$Q = A \cdot v = 0.3\,\text{m}^2 \cdot 0.25\,\text{m/s} = 0.075\,\text{m}^3/s$$

For the dry season:

$$A = w \cdot d = 0.8\,\text{m} \cdot 0.1\,\text{m} = 0.08\,\text{m}^2$$
$$Q = A \cdot v = 0.08\,\text{m}^2 \cdot 0.15\,\text{m/s} = 0.012\,\text{m}^3/s$$

This case study illustrates the significant variation in spring flow between seasons. Such assessments are vital for planning water usage and understanding the sustainability of the spring as a water source.

Conclusion

Assessing the flow and reliability of springs involves careful measurement and monitoring of discharge rates, understanding the factors that influence flow, and maintaining a consistent evaluation of water quality. By employing these techniques, individuals can ensure that springs remain a viable water source in survival situations, providing essential hydration and sanitation needs.

Techniques for Harvesting Water from Springs

Harvesting water from springs can be a reliable and sustainable method of obtaining fresh water in survival situations. Springs are natural outlets where groundwater flows to the surface, often replenished by rainfall or snowmelt. This section outlines several techniques for effectively harvesting water from springs, addressing both the theory behind each method and practical considerations.

Understanding Spring Dynamics

A spring is formed when the water table intersects the land surface, allowing groundwater to flow out. The flow rate and volume of water from a spring can vary based on factors such as:

- **Geological Composition:** The type of soil and rock in the area can influence how easily water can flow through the ground. For example, porous materials like sandstone allow for higher water flow compared to impermeable materials like clay.

SPRINGS AND SEEPS

- **Hydraulic Gradient:** The slope of the water table affects the pressure that drives water to the surface. A steeper gradient can lead to a more vigorous spring.
- **Seasonal Variations:** Springs may exhibit fluctuating flow rates depending on the season, particularly in regions with significant rainfall or snowmelt.

Techniques for Water Harvesting

2.1 Direct Collection The simplest method of harvesting water from a spring is direct collection. This involves positioning a container or reservoir at the spring's outlet to capture the flowing water.

- **Considerations:** Ensure that the container is clean and free from contaminants. Additionally, the collection point should be strategically chosen to avoid debris and sediment.
- **Example:** A hiker can use a collapsible water bag placed directly under a small spring to collect water as it flows out.

2.2 Channeling Water to Storage Tanks For springs with a consistent flow, constructing a channel can facilitate water movement to a storage tank. This method is particularly useful for larger springs.

- **Construction:** Create a shallow trench from the spring to the storage tank, ensuring a gentle slope to allow gravity to assist in water flow. Use materials like stones or plastic lining to prevent erosion.
- **Example:** In rural areas, farmers often build channels to direct spring water into irrigation ponds or cisterns.

2.3 Utilizing a Spring Box A spring box is a structure designed to capture and store spring water while preventing contamination. This technique is ideal for maintaining water quality.

- **Construction:** Build a box around the spring outlet using waterproof materials. The box should have an inlet for water to flow in and an outlet for drawing water out. Ensure that the top is covered to prevent debris from entering.

- **Maintenance:** Regularly check the spring box for sediment buildup and clean it as necessary to ensure optimal water quality.

- **Example:** Many rural communities use spring boxes to provide a reliable water source for households.

2.4 Water Filtration and Purification   Regardless of the harvesting method, it is crucial to purify the water collected from springs to ensure it is safe for consumption. Various purification techniques can be employed:

- **Filtration:** Use a multi-stage filtration system to remove sediments and particles. This can include sand, charcoal, and ceramic filters.

- **Chemical Treatment:** Adding chlorine or iodine can effectively disinfect spring water, killing harmful pathogens.

- **UV Treatment:** Exposing water to ultraviolet light can also purify it by destroying microorganisms.

Challenges and Solutions

While harvesting water from springs can be effective, several challenges may arise:

- **Contamination:** Springs can be susceptible to contamination from surface runoff, animal waste, or human activity. Regular testing for contaminants is essential.

- **Seasonal Flow Variability:** During dry seasons, springs may reduce in flow or dry up completely. It is advisable to monitor the spring's flow rate and develop alternative water sources if necessary.

- **Legal Considerations:** In some regions, water rights and regulations may restrict the use of spring water. Always check local laws before harvesting.

Conclusion

Harvesting water from springs presents an opportunity to access a vital resource in survival situations. By understanding the dynamics of springs and employing various harvesting techniques, individuals can secure a sustainable water supply. However, it is essential to prioritize water quality and be aware of potential challenges. With careful planning and execution, springs can serve as reliable sources of fresh water.

Purifying Spring Water for Consumption

Spring water is often considered one of the most reliable natural water sources due to its flow from underground aquifers, which can filter contaminants through soil and rock. However, it is essential to purify spring water before consumption to ensure it is safe and free from harmful pathogens and pollutants. This section explores various methods for purifying spring water, the underlying theory, potential problems, and practical examples.

Understanding Contaminants in Spring Water

Spring water can contain various contaminants, including:

- **Microbial Contaminants:** Bacteria, viruses, and protozoa can enter spring water through animal waste or surface runoff. Common pathogens include *E. coli*, *Giardia*, and *Cryptosporidium*.

- **Chemical Contaminants:** Pesticides, heavy metals, and other chemicals may leach into spring water from agricultural runoff or industrial activities.

- **Physical Contaminants:** Sediments and particulate matter can affect the clarity and taste of water.

Methods for Purifying Spring Water

1. Filtration Systems Filtration is one of the most straightforward methods for purifying spring water. It involves passing water through a filter that removes sediments and pathogens.

$$\text{Flow Rate} = \frac{\text{Volume of Water}}{\text{Time}} \quad (20)$$

Common filtration methods include:

- **Ceramic Filters:** These filters have small pores that trap bacteria and sediments. They are effective against larger pathogens but may not remove viruses.

- **Activated Carbon Filters:** These filters adsorb chemicals and improve taste. They are less effective against microorganisms unless combined with other methods.

- **Reverse Osmosis:** This method uses a semi-permeable membrane to remove a wide range of contaminants, including dissolved salts and heavy metals.

2. Chemical Treatments Chemical treatments involve adding substances to water to kill pathogens. Common chemicals include:

- **Chlorine:** A widely used disinfectant, effective against bacteria and viruses. The recommended dosage is 2-4 mg/L, with a contact time of at least 30 minutes.

- **Iodine:** Effective against bacteria and viruses, iodine can be used in tablet form or as a tincture. Dosage varies, but a common recommendation is 5-10 drops per quart of water.

- **Hydrogen Peroxide:** This can be used at a concentration of 3

3. UV and Solar Disinfection Ultraviolet (UV) light can effectively kill microorganisms in water. UV disinfection systems expose water to UV light, which damages the DNA of pathogens, rendering them inactive.

$$\text{UV Dose} = \text{Intensity} \times \text{Exposure Time} \tag{21}$$

For effective disinfection, a UV dose of at least 30 mJ/cm^2 is recommended. Solar disinfection (SODIS) utilizes sunlight to purify water in clear plastic bottles. Exposing the bottles to sunlight for 6 hours can effectively kill pathogens.

4. Electrochemical and Membrane Technologies Advanced purification methods include:

- **Electrochemical Disinfection:** This method uses electric current to generate disinfectants in situ, such as chlorine or ozone, effectively killing pathogens.

- **Membrane Technologies:** Techniques like nanofiltration and ultrafiltration can remove pathogens and chemical contaminants, providing a high level of purification.

Practical Examples of Purification

Example 1: Using a Portable Water Filter A hiker discovers a spring while trekking. They use a portable water filter with a ceramic element to remove sediments and bacteria. After filtering, they treat the water with iodine tablets, following the manufacturer's instructions. This dual approach ensures the water is safe for drinking.

Example 2: Solar Disinfection in Emergency Situations   During a camping trip, a group runs out of water and finds a spring. They fill clear plastic bottles with the spring water and leave them in direct sunlight for 6 hours. After this period, they test the water for clarity and odor, finding it suitable for consumption.

Potential Problems and Considerations

While purifying spring water, several challenges may arise:

- **Inconsistent Quality:** The quality of spring water can vary based on environmental factors, such as rainfall and nearby agricultural activities. Regular testing is crucial.

- **Chemical Residues:** Some purification methods may leave chemical residues that can affect taste and safety. It is essential to follow recommended dosages and allow adequate contact time.

- **Equipment Limitations:** Portable filters may not remove all viruses, and UV systems require electricity or sunlight. Always have a backup purification method.

Conclusion

Purifying spring water is a critical step in ensuring safe drinking water in survival situations. By employing a combination of filtration, chemical treatments, UV disinfection, and advanced technologies, individuals can effectively remove contaminants and provide safe water for consumption. Regular testing and awareness of potential challenges will enhance the reliability of spring water as a vital resource in survival scenarios.

Underground Streams and Rivers

Understanding the Formation of Underground Waterways

Underground waterways, often referred to as aquifers or subterranean rivers, are significant sources of fresh water that flow beneath the Earth's surface. Understanding their formation is crucial for effective water harvesting and management. This section delves into the geological and hydrological processes that contribute to the development of these hidden water sources.

Geological Formation

The formation of underground waterways is primarily influenced by geological processes over thousands to millions of years. The key factors include:

- **Rock Type:** The type of rock in a region significantly affects water retention and flow. Porous rocks, such as sandstone and limestone, allow water to seep through and accumulate. In contrast, impermeable rocks, such as granite, hinder water movement.

- **Soil Composition:** The soil layer above the bedrock plays a crucial role in filtering and directing water. Sandy soils facilitate rapid drainage, while clay soils can retain water, creating conditions for underground reservoirs.

- **Tectonic Activity:** Earthquakes and other tectonic activities can create fractures and faults in the Earth's crust, allowing water to flow through these new pathways. This can lead to the formation of underground rivers.

Hydrological Cycle

The hydrological cycle is integral to the formation of underground waterways. The cycle involves the continuous movement of water within the Earth and atmosphere, encompassing processes such as evaporation, condensation, precipitation, infiltration, and runoff.

$$P = E + R + \Delta S \qquad (22)$$

Where:

- P = Precipitation
- E = Evapotranspiration
- R = Runoff
- ΔS = Change in storage (including groundwater)

When precipitation occurs, some of the water infiltrates the ground, replenishing underground reservoirs. The rate of infiltration is influenced by soil permeability and saturation levels, which can vary based on seasonal changes and land use.

Types of Underground Water Sources

There are several types of underground water sources:

- **Unconfined Aquifers:** These aquifers are directly recharged by surface water. They are typically found in areas where the water table is close to the surface, allowing for easy access and extraction.

- **Confined Aquifers:** These are trapped between layers of impermeable rock, creating pressure that can lead to artesian wells. Water in confined aquifers is often older and may contain minerals that affect its quality.

- **Perched Aquifers:** These occur when a layer of impermeable rock or clay creates a localized water table above the main water table. They can be temporary and are often sensitive to changes in rainfall.

Challenges in Understanding Underground Waterways

While understanding the formation of underground waterways is essential, several challenges exist:

- **Limited Visibility:** Unlike surface water, underground waterways are hidden from view, making them difficult to study. This can lead to gaps in knowledge regarding their extent and flow patterns.

- **Pollution Risks:** Underground waterways are susceptible to contamination from surface activities. Understanding the pathways of pollutants is crucial for protecting these vital resources.

- **Over-extraction:** Excessive withdrawal of water from underground sources can lead to depletion and land subsidence, impacting the surrounding ecosystem and human activities.

Real-World Examples

Several notable examples illustrate the formation and significance of underground waterways:

- **The Great Artesian Basin (Australia):** One of the largest confined aquifers in the world, it extends over 1.7 million square kilometers. The basin provides water for agriculture and communities in arid regions, showcasing the importance of understanding and managing underground water sources.

- **The Edwards Aquifer (Texas, USA):** A vital water source for millions, the Edwards Aquifer is characterized by its karst topography, which enhances water flow through limestone formations. Its management is crucial due to the pressures from urban development and agricultural demands.

In conclusion, understanding the formation of underground waterways involves a complex interplay of geological and hydrological processes. Recognizing the types, challenges, and real-world implications of these hidden water sources is essential for effective water management and sustainability. By harnessing this knowledge, individuals and communities can develop strategies for accessing and protecting these vital resources for future generations.

Locating and Accessing Underground Streams

Underground streams, often referred to as subsurface or hyporheic flows, are vital sources of water that can be harnessed for survival in various environments. To effectively locate and access these hidden waterways, one must understand their formation, behavior, and the geological features that influence their presence.

Understanding Underground Streams

Underground streams are formed when surface water infiltrates the ground, moving through soil and rock layers, and eventually flowing through channels in the subsurface. These channels can vary significantly in size and shape, influenced by the geological composition of the area. The presence of permeable materials such as sand, gravel, or fractured rock facilitates the movement of water, while impermeable layers, such as clay or compacted soil, can restrict flow and create pressure zones.

Geological Indicators of Underground Streams

To locate underground streams, one should look for specific geological indicators:

- **Vegetation Patterns:** Areas with lush vegetation or unusually moist soil in otherwise dry conditions may indicate the presence of underground water. Plants such as willows and alders often thrive near underground streams due to their high water needs.

- **Topography:** Low-lying areas, valleys, or depressions in the landscape can suggest the potential for underground water flow. Water tends to accumulate in these areas, and if geological conditions are favorable, it may create underground streams.

- **Soil Composition:** The type of soil present can indicate the likelihood of underground streams. Sandy or loamy soils allow for greater infiltration and water movement compared to clay soils, which are more likely to retain water at the surface.

Techniques for Locating Underground Streams

Several techniques can be employed to locate underground streams effectively:

1. **Geophysical Surveys:** Techniques such as electrical resistivity tomography (ERT) or ground-penetrating radar (GPR) can provide valuable insights into subsurface water flow. ERT measures the resistance of the ground to electrical currents, identifying saturated zones, while GPR uses radar pulses to image the subsurface and detect water channels.

2. **Hydrological Mapping:** Consulting hydrological maps can reveal information about the groundwater flow in the area. These maps often show the locations of known aquifers, springs, and other water sources that can indicate the presence of underground streams.

3. **Observation of Surface Indicators:** Careful observation of surface features, such as springs, seeps, and water pooling, can provide clues about the underground water flow. Noting the direction of surface water flow can help infer the likely path of underground streams.

Accessing Underground Streams

Once an underground stream has been located, accessing it requires specific techniques to ensure efficient water extraction while minimizing environmental impact.

- **Dowsing:** While not scientifically proven, some individuals use dowsing rods to locate underground water sources. This traditional method involves holding two rods and walking over the area, with the rods purportedly moving when over a water source.

- **Digging Test Pits:** If geological indicators suggest the presence of an underground stream, digging test pits can help access the water. It is essential to dig in areas with soft or moist soil, as these are more likely to lead to water.

- **Boreholes:** For a more permanent solution, drilling boreholes can provide access to underground streams. Borehole drilling requires specialized equipment and knowledge of local geology to ensure that the drill reaches the water source without causing contamination.

Challenges in Accessing Underground Streams

Accessing underground streams can present several challenges:

- **Legal Restrictions:** In many regions, accessing underground water may be subject to legal restrictions. It is crucial to understand local water rights and obtain necessary permits before attempting to extract water.

- **Environmental Impact:** Over-extraction of underground water can lead to ecological imbalances. It's important to monitor the extraction rate and ensure it does not exceed the natural recharge rate of the underground stream.

- **Water Quality Concerns:** Water from underground streams may still require purification before use. Contaminants can enter the water source from surface runoff or through the soil, necessitating testing and treatment to ensure safety.

Conclusion

Locating and accessing underground streams is a valuable skill in survival situations. By understanding the geological indicators, employing effective locating techniques, and being mindful of the challenges involved, individuals can successfully tap into these hidden water sources. As always, responsible management and conservation practices should guide any efforts to utilize underground water, ensuring that these vital resources remain available for future generations.

Techniques for Collecting Water from Underground Rivers

Underground rivers represent a significant source of freshwater, often flowing beneath the surface in various geological formations. Collecting water from these hidden waterways requires an understanding of their dynamics, the surrounding environment, and specific techniques tailored to the unique challenges posed by subterranean water sources. This section will explore effective methods for accessing and collecting water from underground rivers, addressing potential problems and providing practical examples.

Understanding the Flow of Underground Rivers

Before attempting to collect water from underground rivers, it is crucial to understand how these waterways function. Underground rivers typically flow through porous rock formations, such as limestone or sandstone, which allow water to move freely while filtering out impurities. The flow rate and volume of water can vary significantly based on geological conditions, seasonal changes, and surrounding environmental factors.

The flow of water in underground rivers can be described by the Darcy's Law equation:

$$Q = k \cdot A \cdot \frac{\Delta h}{L} \qquad (23)$$

Where:

- Q = flow rate (m³/s)
- k = hydraulic conductivity of the material (m/s)
- A = cross-sectional area of flow (m²)
- Δh = difference in hydraulic head (m)
- L = length of flow path (m)

This equation illustrates how the flow of water is influenced by the properties of the underground material, the pressure gradient, and the cross-sectional area of the river. Understanding these variables can help in determining the best techniques for water collection.

Techniques for Collection

There are several methods for collecting water from underground rivers, each with its own advantages and challenges. The choice of technique will depend on the specific conditions of the underground river, including its depth, flow rate, and the surrounding geology.

1. Well Construction Constructing a well is one of the most common methods for accessing underground rivers. A well can tap into the water table or directly into the river itself. The construction involves the following steps:

- **Site Selection:** Choose a location where geological surveys indicate the presence of an underground river. Look for signs of water flow, such as vegetation patterns or animal tracks.

- **Drilling:** Use a hand auger or a powered drill to create a borehole down to the water source. The depth will depend on the water table and the specific geology of the area.

- **Casing:** Install a casing to prevent the walls of the well from collapsing and to keep surface contaminants out of the water supply.

- **Pump Installation:** Depending on the depth of the water, install a hand pump or a powered pump to extract water from the well.

2. **Siphoning Techniques** Siphoning is a method that can be used when the underground river is accessible from a lower elevation. This technique utilizes gravity to move water from the river to the surface:

- **Materials Needed:** A length of flexible tubing (such as PVC or rubber) is required for siphoning.

- **Setup:** Insert one end of the tubing into the underground river, ensuring it is submerged. The other end should be positioned at a lower elevation where water is to be collected.

- **Creating a Siphon:** To initiate the siphon, fill the tubing with water and then quickly place your thumb over one end. Lower the thumbed end below the water level, release your thumb, and the water will flow through the tubing due to atmospheric pressure and gravity.

3. **Subsurface Drainage Systems** In situations where the underground river is not easily accessible, subsurface drainage systems can be employed to collect water. This method involves creating a network of trenches or perforated pipes that capture groundwater as it flows towards the surface:

- **Trench Design:** Dig trenches that intercept the flow of the underground river. The trenches should be sloped to encourage water movement toward a collection point.

- **Pipe Installation:** Lay perforated pipes at the bottom of the trenches to facilitate water collection. Ensure that the pipes are covered with gravel to filter out sediments.

- **Collection Basin:** Direct the water from the pipes into a collection basin or tank for storage and further use.

4. **Natural Springs** In some cases, underground rivers may surface as natural springs. These springs can be identified by observing areas of consistent moisture or vegetation. Collecting water from springs involves:

- **Identification:** Look for signs of water bubbling to the surface, often found in low-lying areas or along hillsides.
- **Collection Method:** Create a small catchment area around the spring to collect water. This can be done by digging a shallow basin or using containers to capture the flow.
- **Purification:** Since spring water may contain contaminants, it is essential to purify it using filtration or boiling methods before consumption.

Challenges and Considerations

While collecting water from underground rivers can be rewarding, there are several challenges to consider:

- **Water Quality:** Underground rivers may carry pollutants or pathogens. Regular testing and purification are necessary to ensure water safety.
- **Legal Regulations:** Be aware of local laws regarding water rights and extraction. Unauthorized collection can lead to legal issues.
- **Environmental Impact:** Over-extraction from underground rivers can lead to depletion of local aquifers and affect surrounding ecosystems. Sustainable practices should be prioritized.

Examples of Successful Collection Techniques

Several communities worldwide have successfully implemented techniques for collecting water from underground rivers. For instance:

- In rural areas of Mexico, many families rely on traditional well construction methods to access groundwater, ensuring they have a reliable water source throughout the year.

- In parts of Australia, farmers use siphoning techniques to draw water from underground rivers during dry seasons, allowing them to maintain their crops with minimal environmental impact.

- In regions with abundant natural springs, communities have developed catchment systems that not only provide drinking water but also support local agriculture.

In conclusion, collecting water from underground rivers involves a variety of techniques that can be tailored to specific conditions. By understanding the flow dynamics, employing suitable methods, and considering potential challenges, individuals and communities can effectively harness this vital resource for their survival and well-being.

Enhancing Water Flow in Underground Channels

Underground water channels, such as aquifers and subterranean rivers, can serve as vital sources of water in survival situations. However, the natural flow of water through these channels can be influenced by various factors, including geological formations, sediment types, and human interventions. Enhancing water flow in these underground channels can significantly improve water accessibility and sustainability. This section explores methods for enhancing water flow, the underlying theories, potential problems, and practical examples.

Understanding Hydraulic Conductivity

The flow of water through underground channels is governed by Darcy's Law, which states that the flow rate (Q) through a porous medium is proportional to the hydraulic gradient (i) and the cross-sectional area (A) of the flow path:

$$Q = k \cdot A \cdot i \qquad (24)$$

Where:

- Q = Flow rate (m³/s)

- k = Hydraulic conductivity (m/s)

- A = Cross-sectional area (m²)

- i = Hydraulic gradient (dimensionless)

UNDERGROUND STREAMS AND RIVERS

Hydraulic conductivity (k) is a measure of a material's ability to transmit water and is influenced by factors such as soil texture, structure, and saturation levels. Enhancing water flow in underground channels often involves increasing k or optimizing the hydraulic gradient.

Methods for Enhancing Water Flow

1. Excavation and Channel Modification

One of the most direct methods for enhancing water flow is through the excavation of existing underground channels. This can involve the removal of sediment or debris that may be obstructing flow. Additionally, modifying the channel shape can create a more efficient flow path. For example, a wider channel can reduce resistance and increase flow rates.

> **Example**
>
> In a region with clay-rich soil, excavating a channel and lining it with gravel can significantly enhance water flow. The gravel provides a higher hydraulic conductivity compared to clay, allowing for more efficient water movement.

2. Installation of Permeable Barriers

Permeable barriers can be constructed using materials such as sandbags filled with gravel or geotextiles. These barriers can redirect water flow towards desired areas, enhancing the overall water availability in specific locations.

> **Example**
>
> In a drought-prone area, installing a permeable barrier along the edge of an underground stream can help capture and concentrate water flow, making it easier to access during dry periods.

3. Use of Water Retention Structures

Constructing water retention structures, such as percolation ponds or catchment systems, can help manage and enhance underground water flow. These structures allow for the gradual infiltration of water into the ground, increasing the recharge rate of underground channels.

> **Example**
>
> A percolation pond designed to capture runoff from rainfall can enhance the recharge of an adjacent aquifer, effectively increasing the amount of water available for extraction.

4. Creating Recharge Zones

Establishing recharge zones where water can infiltrate the ground can significantly enhance flow in underground channels. This can involve planting vegetation that promotes water absorption or amending the soil to increase its permeability.

> **Example**
>
> In agricultural areas, creating recharge zones by planting deep-rooted crops can help enhance water flow into underground channels, especially during irrigation periods.

Potential Problems and Considerations

While enhancing water flow in underground channels can provide significant benefits, several challenges and considerations must be addressed:

- **Environmental Impact:** Modifying natural water flow can disrupt local ecosystems. It is crucial to assess the potential impact on flora and fauna before implementing enhancements.

- **Sustainability:** Enhancing water flow should not lead to over-extraction. Sustainable practices must be employed to ensure that water resources are not depleted.

- **Legal and Regulatory Issues:** Water rights and regulations may limit the ability to modify underground channels. It is essential to consult local regulations and obtain necessary permits.

Conclusion

Enhancing water flow in underground channels is a critical strategy for improving water accessibility in survival situations. By understanding the principles of hydraulic conductivity and employing various methods such as excavation, permeable barriers, and recharge zones, individuals can significantly increase their chances of obtaining water from hidden underground sources. However, it is vital to approach these enhancements with a consideration for environmental impact, sustainability, and legal regulations.

Percolation Ponds and Catchments

Designing and Building Percolation Ponds

Percolation ponds, also known as infiltration basins, are engineered structures that allow surface water to percolate into the ground, replenishing groundwater supplies while providing a means for water storage. This section outlines the essential steps in designing and constructing percolation ponds, including considerations of site selection, design principles, construction techniques, and maintenance practices.

Understanding Percolation Ponds

Percolation ponds are designed to capture runoff from rainfall or melting snow, allowing it to seep into the soil rather than being lost to evaporation or surface runoff. These ponds serve multiple purposes, including groundwater recharge, flood control, and habitat creation for local wildlife. The effectiveness of a percolation pond is influenced by soil type, topography, and local climate conditions.

Site Selection

The first step in building a percolation pond is selecting an appropriate site. Factors to consider include:

- **Soil Permeability:** Conduct a percolation test to determine the rate at which water infiltrates the soil. Sandy soils have high permeability, making them ideal for percolation ponds, while clayey soils may hinder infiltration.

- **Topography:** Choose a location that naturally collects runoff, such as low-lying areas or depressions. The pond should be positioned to maximize water flow into it.

- **Proximity to Water Sources:** Ensure that the pond is located near a reliable source of runoff, such as a drainage area or a roof catchment system.

- **Environmental Impact:** Assess the potential impact on local ecosystems, ensuring that the pond does not disrupt wildlife habitats or water quality in nearby streams or rivers.

Design Principles

Once a suitable site is identified, the next step is to design the percolation pond. Key design principles include:

- **Size and Depth:** The size of the pond should be proportional to the area of land that drains into it. A common guideline is to design the pond to be at least 10% of the contributing drainage area. The depth should typically range from 1 to 3 meters, depending on soil type and local conditions.

- **Shape:** A larger surface area allows for greater evaporation and infiltration. Oval or rectangular shapes are often preferred, as they provide a larger perimeter relative to the area.

- **Inlet and Outlet Structures:** Design inlet structures to control the flow of water into the pond, preventing erosion and sediment buildup. Outlet structures should allow for controlled drainage while preventing the loss of water through surface runoff.

The design can be mathematically represented by the following equation for estimating the required pond area A based on the drainage area D and the desired pond-to-drainage area ratio R:

$$A = R \times D \qquad (25)$$

Where:

- A = Area of the percolation pond (m²)
- R = Pond-to-drainage area ratio (unitless)
- D = Area of the contributing drainage area (m²)

Construction Techniques

The construction of a percolation pond involves several steps:

1. **Excavation:** Clear the site of vegetation and debris, and excavate the area to the desired depth. Ensure that the sides of the pond are sloped to prevent erosion.

2. **Soil Preparation:** If necessary, amend the soil to enhance permeability. This may involve mixing in sand or gravel to improve drainage.

3. **Installation of Inlet and Outlet Structures:** Construct inlet and outlet structures using materials such as concrete or stone. Ensure that these structures are properly anchored and designed to handle expected water flows.

4. **Landscaping:** After excavation, landscape the surrounding area to promote vegetation growth, which helps stabilize the soil and provides natural filtration.

Maintenance Practices

To ensure the long-term effectiveness of a percolation pond, regular maintenance is essential. Key maintenance practices include:

- **Regular Inspections:** Conduct periodic inspections to check for erosion, sediment buildup, and vegetation health. Remove debris and sediment as needed to maintain water flow.

- **Vegetation Management:** Encourage native plants around the pond to enhance filtration and provide habitat. Avoid invasive species that may disrupt the ecosystem.

- **Water Quality Monitoring:** Regularly test the water quality to ensure that it remains suitable for groundwater recharge. This may involve checking for contaminants or changes in pH levels.

Challenges and Solutions

While designing and building percolation ponds can be highly effective, several challenges may arise:

- **Poor Soil Permeability:** If the soil has low permeability, consider amending it or constructing a lined pond to prevent water loss.

- **Erosion:** Implement erosion control measures, such as vegetation planting or installing riprap along the edges of the pond.

- **Sediment Accumulation:** Regularly remove sediment to maintain the pond's capacity and effectiveness. Design the inlet to minimize sediment transport into the pond.

In conclusion, designing and building percolation ponds requires careful consideration of site selection, design principles, construction techniques, and ongoing maintenance. By following these guidelines, individuals can create effective water harvesting systems that contribute to sustainable water management and groundwater recharge.

Determining Suitable Catchment Areas

In the context of rainwater harvesting, identifying suitable catchment areas is critical for maximizing water collection efficiency. A catchment area, also known as a drainage basin, is the land area from which rainfall flows into a particular water collection system. The effectiveness of a rainwater harvesting system largely depends on the size, shape, and characteristics of the catchment area.

Factors Influencing Catchment Area Selection

Several factors must be considered when determining suitable catchment areas:

- **Topography:** The slope and elevation of the land influence how water flows. Steeper slopes can lead to faster runoff, while flatter areas may allow water to pool. It is essential to analyze the topography using contour maps or digital elevation models (DEMs) to identify optimal locations for catchment.

- **Soil Type:** The permeability of the soil affects how much water can be absorbed versus how much will run off. Sandy soils, for example, allow for greater infiltration, while clay soils may lead to more runoff due to their lower permeability. Soil tests can help determine the infiltration rate, which is crucial for estimating the potential water yield from the catchment area.

- **Vegetation Cover:** Areas with dense vegetation can intercept rainfall and reduce runoff, while bare soil may lead to increased erosion and reduced water collection efficiency. Assessing the type and density of vegetation can help in understanding how much rainfall can be effectively captured.

PERCOLATION PONDS AND CATCHMENTS

- **Land Use:** Urban areas with impervious surfaces (e.g., roads, buildings) tend to have higher runoff rates compared to rural areas. Understanding land use patterns can assist in predicting water flow dynamics and potential catchment yields.

- **Climate:** Regional climatic conditions, including average rainfall, seasonal variations, and evaporation rates, must be considered. Historical weather data can provide insights into the expected rainfall patterns and help in designing an effective catchment system.

Calculating Catchment Area

To quantify the potential yield from a catchment area, the following equation can be employed:

$$V = A \times P \times E \qquad (26)$$

where:

- V = Volume of water collected (in cubic meters)
- A = Area of the catchment (in square meters)
- P = Average annual precipitation (in meters)
- E = Efficiency factor (expressed as a decimal, accounting for losses due to evaporation, infiltration, and other factors)

For example, if a catchment area measures $500\,\text{m}^2$, the average annual precipitation is $1.2\,\text{m}$, and the efficiency factor is estimated at 0.75:

$$V = 500\,\text{m}^2 \times 1.2\,\text{m} \times 0.75 = 450\,\text{m}^3 \qquad (27)$$

This calculation indicates that approximately $450\,\text{m}^3$ of water could be harvested from this catchment area annually.

Examples of Suitable Catchment Areas

1. **Rooftops:** Urban environments often utilize rooftops as catchment areas. A flat roof with a smooth surface can efficiently collect rainwater. The area of the roof, along with local precipitation data, can be used to estimate potential water yield.

2. **Natural Basins:** In rural settings, natural depressions or basins can serve as effective catchment areas. These areas can be enhanced by constructing small embankments to retain water and direct it towards storage systems.

3. **Agricultural Fields:** Fields can be designed with contour plowing or terracing to create effective catchment areas. These methods help slow down water flow and increase infiltration, allowing more water to be absorbed by the soil and collected in percolation ponds.

Challenges in Identifying Suitable Catchment Areas

Identifying suitable catchment areas is not without challenges:

- **Environmental Impact:** Altering natural landscapes to create catchment areas can have ecological consequences, such as habitat destruction and increased erosion. It is crucial to evaluate the environmental impact before making modifications.

- **Regulatory Restrictions:** Local regulations may limit the types of modifications that can be made to land for water harvesting purposes. It is essential to consult local authorities to ensure compliance with zoning laws and environmental regulations.

- **Seasonal Variability:** Seasonal variations in rainfall can affect the reliability of catchment areas. Areas that may seem suitable during wet seasons could become less effective during droughts. Continuous monitoring and adaptive management strategies are necessary to optimize water collection.

In conclusion, determining suitable catchment areas requires a comprehensive understanding of various factors, including topography, soil type, vegetation, land use, and climate. By carefully analyzing these elements and utilizing mathematical calculations to estimate potential yields, individuals can design effective rainwater harvesting systems that maximize water collection while minimizing environmental impact.

Utilizing Percolation Ponds and Catchments for Long-term Water Storage

Percolation ponds and catchments serve as crucial components in sustainable water management, particularly in arid and semi-arid regions where surface water is scarce. These systems not only capture and store water but also enhance

PERCOLATION PONDS AND CATCHMENTS

groundwater recharge, ensuring a steady supply of water for various uses. This section delves into the design, implementation, and maintenance of percolation ponds and catchments, providing actionable insights for maximizing their efficiency.

Designing and Building Percolation Ponds

The design of a percolation pond is influenced by several factors, including local topography, soil type, and hydrological conditions. A well-designed percolation pond should facilitate maximum water infiltration while minimizing evaporation losses. The following steps outline the design process:

1. **Site Selection:** Choose a location that naturally collects runoff water. Ideal sites are typically low-lying areas with permeable soils that allow for efficient water absorption.

2. **Sizing the Pond:** The surface area of the pond should be calculated based on the expected volume of runoff and the infiltration rate of the soil. The equation for determining the required surface area A is given by:

$$A = \frac{V}{I}$$

   where V is the volume of water to be stored (in cubic meters) and I is the infiltration rate (in cubic meters per square meter per day).

3. **Shape and Depth:** Design the pond with a shallow basin to reduce evaporation. A depth of 1 to 2 meters is generally sufficient, allowing for adequate water storage while promoting vegetation growth around the edges.

Determining Suitable Catchment Areas

Catchment areas are critical for directing water into percolation ponds. The effectiveness of a catchment area can be evaluated through the following considerations:

- **Topography:** Utilize natural slopes to channel water towards the pond. The catchment area should ideally have a gradient of at least 2-5% to facilitate runoff.

- **Soil Type:** Assess the soil's permeability; sandy and loamy soils are preferable for catchment areas, as they allow for quick infiltration.

- **Vegetation:** Maintain vegetation cover to reduce erosion and improve water retention. Native plants can also enhance biodiversity and provide additional benefits to the ecosystem.

Utilizing Percolation Ponds and Catchments for Long-term Water Storage

Once constructed, percolation ponds and catchments can be utilized for long-term water storage through the following methods:

1. **Water Harvesting:** During rainy seasons, capture and direct runoff into the percolation pond. Implementing swales or berms can help channel water effectively.

2. **Groundwater Recharge:** The water stored in percolation ponds gradually infiltrates the ground, recharging local aquifers. This process can be enhanced by maintaining a healthy surrounding ecosystem that supports soil structure and permeability.

3. **Water Quality Management:** Regularly monitor the water quality in percolation ponds to prevent contamination. Implementing natural filtration systems using gravel and vegetation can help maintain water purity.

Building Effective Rainwater Harvesting Systems

Integrating rainwater harvesting systems with percolation ponds can significantly enhance water storage capabilities. The following strategies can be employed:

- **Collection Systems:** Install gutters and downspouts on buildings to direct rainwater into storage tanks or directly into percolation ponds.

- **Storage Tanks:** Use underground tanks to store collected rainwater before it is directed to the percolation pond. This method can help manage water availability during dry periods.

- **Filtration:** Implement filtration systems to remove debris and contaminants from rainwater before it enters the pond, ensuring the quality of stored water.

Challenges and Considerations

While percolation ponds and catchments are effective for water storage, several challenges must be addressed:

- **Evaporation Losses:** In hot climates, evaporation can significantly reduce water levels. Consider planting vegetation around the pond to provide shade and reduce evaporation.

- **Sedimentation:** Over time, sediments can accumulate in the pond, reducing its capacity. Regular maintenance, including dredging, is essential to maintain functionality.

- **Regulatory Compliance:** Ensure that the construction and operation of percolation ponds comply with local water management regulations. Consult local authorities for guidance on permits and legal considerations.

In conclusion, percolation ponds and catchments offer a sustainable solution for long-term water storage, particularly in regions facing water scarcity. By implementing effective design strategies, integrating rainwater harvesting, and addressing potential challenges, individuals and communities can significantly enhance their water resilience and sustainability.

Building Effective Rainwater Harvesting Systems

Rainwater harvesting systems are essential for capturing and utilizing the natural precipitation that falls on your property. These systems can provide a sustainable source of water for various uses, including irrigation, toilet flushing, and even potable water when properly treated. This section will discuss the key components of an effective rainwater harvesting system, including design considerations, materials, and maintenance practices.

System Design

The design of a rainwater harvesting system involves several critical components:

1. **Catchment Area:** The surface area from which rainwater is collected. This is typically the roof of a building, which should be made of non-toxic materials to ensure water quality. The catchment area should be smooth and clean to minimize debris and contaminants.

2. **Gutters and Downspouts:** These are essential for directing rainwater from the catchment area to the storage system. Gutters should be sized appropriately to handle peak rainfall events, typically following the formula:

$$Q = A \cdot C \cdot I \qquad (28)$$

where Q is the runoff (in liters), A is the catchment area (in square meters), C is the runoff coefficient (dimensionless, dependent on the material), and I is the rainfall intensity (in mm/h).

3. **First Flush Diverters:** These devices are designed to divert the initial flow of rainwater, which may contain contaminants from the roof. A first flush system typically consists of a collection chamber that fills with the first few liters of rainwater, allowing cleaner water to flow into the storage tank.

4. **Storage Tanks:** The tanks should be made of materials that do not leach harmful substances into the water. Common materials include polyethylene, fiberglass, or concrete. The size of the storage tank can be estimated based on the average rainfall and the catchment area:

$$V = R \cdot A \qquad (29)$$

where V is the volume of water collected (in liters), R is the average rainfall (in meters), and A is the catchment area (in square meters).

5. **Filtration and Treatment:** To ensure the water is safe for use, it may need to be filtered and treated. This can include sediment filters, activated carbon filters, and UV disinfection systems, depending on the intended use of the water.

Materials and Construction

When constructing a rainwater harvesting system, the choice of materials is crucial for ensuring durability and effectiveness. Here are some recommended materials:

- **Gutters:** Use aluminum or PVC gutters, which are lightweight, durable, and resistant to corrosion.
- **Storage Tanks:** Choose food-grade polyethylene tanks for potable water or galvanized steel for non-potable applications. Ensure that all tanks are covered to prevent mosquito breeding and contamination.

- **Filters:** Use high-quality sediment filters and UV disinfection units to ensure water quality. Regular maintenance and replacement of filters are essential to keep the system functioning effectively.

Maintenance Practices

To ensure the longevity and efficiency of your rainwater harvesting system, regular maintenance is required. Consider the following practices:

- **Regular Inspections:** Inspect gutters, downspouts, and filters for debris and blockages at least twice a year. Clean them as necessary to ensure optimal water flow.
- **Tank Cleaning:** Clean the storage tank annually to remove sediment and biofilm that may accumulate over time. This will help maintain water quality and prevent odors.
- **Monitoring Water Quality:** Test the water quality periodically for contaminants, especially if the water is intended for potable use. This can include testing for bacteria, heavy metals, and chemical pollutants.

Case Study: Successful Implementation

A successful example of a rainwater harvesting system can be found in the community of EcoVillage in Ithaca, New York. Residents have implemented a community-wide rainwater harvesting program that captures rainwater from roofs and directs it into a centralized storage system. The harvested rainwater is treated and used for irrigation and non-potable purposes throughout the community.

The system's design includes:

- A large catchment area consisting of multiple roofs.
- A network of gutters and downspouts connected to a central storage tank with a capacity of 50,000 liters.
- A first flush diverter to ensure clean water is collected.
- A filtration system that includes sediment filters and UV disinfection for safe water usage.

The community has reported a significant reduction in water bills and has increased its resilience to drought conditions by utilizing harvested rainwater effectively.

Conclusion

Building an effective rainwater harvesting system is an invaluable investment in water sustainability. By carefully designing the system, selecting appropriate materials, and maintaining the system regularly, individuals and communities can harness the power of rainwater to meet their water needs. This not only conserves water resources but also enhances self-sufficiency and resilience in the face of changing climate conditions.

Constructing Underground Water Storage Systems

Building Cisterns and Wells

Selecting the Right Location for Your Cistern or Well

Selecting the appropriate location for a cistern or well is a critical step in ensuring a reliable and sustainable water supply. The choice of location can significantly affect the quality, quantity, and accessibility of water. This section will explore various factors to consider when choosing a site for your cistern or well, including geological, hydrological, and environmental considerations.

Geological Considerations

The geological characteristics of the site play a vital role in determining the feasibility of constructing a well or cistern. Key geological factors include:

- **Soil Type:** The type of soil influences water retention and drainage capabilities. Sandy soils, for instance, allow for rapid drainage but may not retain water effectively, while clay soils retain water but can impede drainage. A mixed soil profile often provides a balance of these properties.

- **Bedrock Composition:** The presence of bedrock can limit the depth of a well. It is essential to understand the type of bedrock in your area, as some types (e.g., limestone) are more conducive to groundwater accumulation than others (e.g., granite).

- **Slope and Topography:** The slope of the land affects water runoff and drainage patterns. Ideally, a well should be located on a gentle slope to facilitate water movement toward the well while avoiding areas prone to flooding.

Hydrological Considerations

Understanding the hydrology of the area is crucial for selecting a suitable location for a cistern or well. Consider the following hydrological factors:

- **Water Table Depth:** The depth of the water table can vary significantly depending on geographical location, season, and weather conditions. It is essential to conduct a water table survey to determine the average depth in your area. A well should ideally be drilled to a depth where it can access a reliable source of groundwater.

- **Proximity to Surface Water:** While surface water sources (like rivers or lakes) can indicate the presence of groundwater, they can also pose contamination risks. A safe distance from surface water should be maintained to minimize the risk of pollution.

- **Recharge Areas:** Identifying areas where groundwater recharge occurs is essential for sustainable water sourcing. Recharge areas are typically characterized by permeable soils and vegetation that facilitate water infiltration. Locating your well near these areas can ensure a more consistent water supply.

Environmental Considerations

Environmental factors must also be taken into account when selecting a location for your cistern or well:

- **Vegetation:** The presence of certain types of vegetation can indicate the availability of groundwater. For example, willow trees and cattails often thrive near water sources. Observing plant life can provide clues about the underlying water table.

- **Wildlife Activity:** Animal activity can also indicate the presence of water. Frequent animal tracks or signs near a location may suggest a reliable water source. However, be cautious, as wildlife can also introduce contaminants.

- **Land Use:** Consider the surrounding land use when selecting your site. Areas near agricultural lands may be subject to pesticide runoff, while industrial

BUILDING CISTERNS AND WELLS

zones may have higher contamination risks. It is crucial to ensure that the location is away from potential sources of pollution.

Practical Examples

To illustrate the importance of selecting the right location, consider the following examples:

- **Example 1: Successful Well Installation** A homeowner in a rural area conducted a thorough geological survey and found a location with sandy loam soil, a shallow water table, and proximity to a natural recharge area. The well was drilled successfully, providing a reliable water source for irrigation and household use.

- **Example 2: Failed Well Installation** In contrast, another homeowner drilled a well near a river without considering the water table depth. The well was too shallow and quickly ran dry during the dry season, leading to costly repairs and a need for an alternative water source.

Conclusion

Selecting the right location for a cistern or well requires careful consideration of geological, hydrological, and environmental factors. Conducting thorough research and possibly consulting local experts can help ensure that your water source is reliable and sustainable. By understanding the dynamics of your chosen site, you can avoid common pitfalls and secure a vital resource for your needs.

$$Q = A \times v \qquad (30)$$

where Q is the flow rate, A is the cross-sectional area of the aquifer, and v is the velocity of groundwater flow. This equation underscores the importance of understanding the hydrological characteristics of your site, as it directly impacts water availability.

In summary, the location of your cistern or well is a foundational aspect of water harvesting. By carefully analyzing the geological, hydrological, and environmental factors, you can optimize your chances of securing a reliable water source for survival and sustainability.

Construction Materials and Techniques for Cisterns

Cisterns are vital structures used for the collection and storage of water, particularly in areas where water scarcity is a concern. The construction of a cistern involves careful selection of materials and techniques to ensure durability, safety, and efficiency. This section outlines the most suitable materials for cistern construction, the techniques involved, and common challenges faced during the process.

Materials for Cistern Construction

The choice of materials for constructing a cistern is crucial. The materials must be durable, non-toxic, and capable of withstanding the pressure of the stored water. Below are some commonly used materials:

- **Concrete:** Concrete is one of the most popular materials for cistern construction due to its strength and durability. It can be poured into molds to create custom shapes and sizes. However, it is essential to use a waterproof concrete mix to prevent leakage and water loss.

- **Steel:** Steel cisterns are often used for their strength and ability to withstand high pressure. They are typically coated with a rust-resistant finish to prolong their lifespan. However, steel can corrode over time if not properly maintained.

- **Plastic (Polyethylene):** Plastic cisterns are lightweight and easy to install. They are resistant to corrosion and can be molded into various shapes. However, they may not be as durable as concrete or steel, especially under extreme temperatures.

- **Fiberglass:** Fiberglass cisterns are strong, lightweight, and resistant to corrosion. They can be manufactured in various sizes and shapes, making them versatile for different applications. However, they can be more expensive than other materials.

- **Brick and Mortar:** Traditional brick and mortar can be used to construct cisterns, especially in areas where these materials are readily available. While they provide excellent insulation and durability, they may require more maintenance to prevent leaks.

BUILDING CISTERNS AND WELLS

Construction Techniques

The construction of a cistern involves several key steps that must be followed to ensure the structure is effective and safe for water storage. Here are the essential techniques:

1. **Site Selection:** The first step in constructing a cistern is selecting an appropriate site. The site should be located away from potential contaminants such as sewage or agricultural runoff. Additionally, the ground should be stable and able to support the weight of the cistern when filled with water.

2. **Excavation:** Once the site is selected, excavation is necessary to create a pit for the cistern. The size of the pit will depend on the desired capacity of the cistern. The depth should be sufficient to accommodate the materials being used and to provide stability.

3. **Foundation:** A solid foundation is crucial for the longevity of the cistern. For concrete cisterns, a base layer of gravel can be laid to promote drainage and prevent settling. For other materials, ensure the foundation is level and well-compacted.

4. **Wall Construction:** The walls of the cistern should be constructed according to the chosen material. For concrete, forms should be set up, and the concrete poured and cured. For brick or block construction, mortar should be applied between bricks, ensuring a watertight seal.

5. **Roofing:** A roof is often necessary to prevent debris from entering the cistern. This can be constructed from the same material as the walls or from a different, lightweight material. Ensure that the roof is designed to handle local weather conditions, including snow loads if applicable.

6. **Sealing:** After construction, it is essential to seal the cistern to prevent leaks. For concrete cisterns, a waterproof sealant can be applied to the interior walls. For other materials, ensure that joints and seams are tightly sealed to prevent water loss.

7. **Inlet and Outlet Installation:** Install a system for water intake and drainage. This may include pipes, valves, and screens to filter out debris. Ensure that the inlet is positioned to collect rainwater effectively while the outlet allows for easy access to stored water.

Common Problems and Solutions

While constructing a cistern, several challenges may arise. Understanding these potential problems and having solutions ready can help ensure the success of the project.

- **Leakage:** Leakage is one of the most common issues faced with cisterns. This can be caused by poor sealing or cracks in the structure. Regular inspections should be conducted, and any leaks should be repaired immediately using appropriate sealants or patches.

- **Contamination:** Contaminants can enter the cistern through the inlet. To minimize this risk, install screens and filters on the inlet to catch debris and prevent contaminants from entering the water supply. Additionally, maintain a clean area around the cistern.

- **Structural Failure:** If the cistern is not constructed properly, it may collapse under the weight of the water. To prevent this, ensure that the foundation is solid and that the walls are built to withstand the pressure of the stored water. Regular maintenance checks should also be conducted.

- **Algae Growth:** Stagnant water in the cistern can lead to algae growth, which can contaminate the water. To combat this, ensure that the cistern is covered and that water is used regularly to prevent stagnation. Consider using UV light or other treatments to control algae.

- **Freezing:** In colder climates, water in cisterns can freeze, which can damage the structure. Insulating the cistern and burying it below the frost line can help mitigate this issue. Additionally, using heating elements or thermal blankets can provide further protection.

Conclusion

Constructing a cistern is a practical solution for water storage in various environments. By selecting the right materials and employing effective construction techniques, you can create a durable and efficient water storage system. Addressing common problems proactively will further enhance the longevity and reliability of your cistern, ensuring that you have access to vital water resources when needed.

Maintaining and Upkeeping Your Cistern or Well

Maintaining and upkeeping your cistern or well is crucial for ensuring a reliable and safe water supply. Regular maintenance helps to prevent contamination, prolongs the lifespan of the system, and ensures that water quality meets health standards. This section outlines essential maintenance practices, common problems, and practical solutions for both cisterns and wells.

Regular Inspections

Regular inspections are the cornerstone of effective maintenance. It is advisable to conduct inspections at least twice a year. During these inspections, check for:

- **Structural Integrity:** Examine the walls, roof, and floor of the cistern or well for cracks, leaks, or signs of deterioration. Pay special attention to the joints where different materials meet.

- **Debris Accumulation:** Remove any debris, leaves, or sediment that may have accumulated inside the cistern or well. This can lead to contamination and reduced water quality.

- **Water Level:** Monitor the water level to ensure it is consistent with expected levels based on seasonal variations and water usage.

- **Signs of Contamination:** Look for any unusual odors, discoloration, or floating particles in the water, which may indicate contamination.

Cleaning Procedures

Cleaning your cistern or well is essential to maintain water quality. The cleaning frequency depends on the volume of water used and the surrounding environment, but it is generally recommended to clean cisterns annually and wells every few years.

Cistern Cleaning:

1. **Drain the Cistern:** Before cleaning, drain the cistern completely. Use a submersible pump to remove the water efficiently.

2. **Scrub the Interior:** Use a mixture of water and a non-toxic cleaning agent to scrub the interior surfaces. A long-handled brush can help reach difficult areas. Pay special attention to corners and edges where algae may accumulate.

3. **Rinse Thoroughly:** After scrubbing, rinse the cistern with clean water to remove any cleaning residues.

4. **Disinfect:** After rinsing, disinfect the cistern using a solution of unscented bleach (5-10

Well Cleaning: Cleaning a well is more complex and often requires professional assistance. However, homeowners can perform basic maintenance:

1. **Remove Debris:** Ensure that the wellhead is clear of debris, vegetation, and other materials that could fall into the well.

2. **Well Disinfection:** Similar to cisterns, wells can be disinfected with bleach. The amount depends on the well's depth and diameter. A common method involves calculating the volume of the well using the formula:

$$V = \pi r^2 h \tag{31}$$

where V is the volume, r is the radius of the well, and h is the height of the water column. The necessary amount of bleach can then be added based on this volume.

Monitoring Water Quality

Water quality should be tested regularly, especially if there are concerns about contamination. Key parameters to test include:

- **Microbial Contaminants:** Test for bacteria such as E. coli and coliforms. A safe level is zero detectable colonies in a 100 mL sample.

- **Chemical Contaminants:** Regularly check for nitrates, heavy metals, and other harmful chemicals. The EPA provides maximum contaminant levels (MCLs) for various substances.

- **pH Levels:** Maintain a pH level between 6.5 and 8.5 for optimal water quality. A pH outside this range can indicate contamination or the need for further treatment.

Common Problems and Solutions

Contamination: Contamination can arise from various sources, including agricultural runoff, septic systems, or surface water infiltration. To mitigate this risk:

- **Proper Wellhead Protection:** Ensure that the wellhead is sealed and elevated to prevent surface water from entering.

- **Distance from Contaminants:** Maintain a safe distance from potential contamination sources, such as septic tanks (at least 50 feet) and livestock areas.

Low Water Levels: Low water levels can indicate over-extraction or drought conditions. To address this:

- **Water Conservation:** Implement water-saving practices to reduce demand.

- **Recharge Techniques:** Consider rainwater harvesting or constructing percolation ponds to enhance groundwater recharge.

Structural Issues: Cracks or leaks in the cistern or well can lead to significant problems. To resolve these issues:

- **Seal Cracks:** Use appropriate sealants or patches to repair cracks. For larger structural issues, consult a professional.

- **Regular Maintenance:** Schedule regular inspections to catch and address problems early.

Conclusion

Maintaining and upkeeping your cistern or well is a proactive approach to ensuring a sustainable and safe water supply. Regular inspections, cleaning, and monitoring water quality are essential practices that help to prevent contamination and prolong the lifespan of your water system. By being aware of common problems and implementing effective solutions, you can secure a reliable source of water for your needs.

Retrofitting Existing Structures for Water Storage

Retrofitting existing structures for water storage is a practical and resourceful approach to enhance water availability, especially in areas where constructing new systems may be impractical or costly. This section explores the principles, methods, and considerations involved in retrofitting various types of structures to serve as effective water storage solutions.

Theoretical Foundations

The fundamental concept behind retrofitting is to utilize available space within existing structures—such as basements, garages, or even old tanks—to create efficient water storage systems. This not only maximizes the use of current resources but also minimizes environmental impact by reducing the need for new materials and construction.

The efficiency of a water storage system can be expressed using the following equation for the volume of water stored:

$$V = A \times h \qquad (32)$$

where V is the volume of water (in cubic meters), A is the surface area of the storage container (in square meters), and h is the height of the water column (in meters). Understanding this relationship helps in determining the capacity of the retrofitted structure.

Identifying Suitable Structures

The first step in retrofitting is identifying which existing structures can be converted into water storage systems. Common candidates include:

- **Basements**: Often underutilized, basements can be equipped with large tanks or cisterns to collect and store water.

- **Sheds and Garages**: These structures can be modified to include storage tanks, especially if they are insulated to prevent freezing in colder climates.

- **Old Water Tanks**: Decommissioned water tanks can be cleaned and repurposed for storage, provided they meet health and safety standards.

- **Bioswales and Rain Gardens**: These landscape features can be retrofitted to include underground storage systems that capture runoff.

Challenges in Retrofitting

While retrofitting offers numerous advantages, it also presents challenges that need to be addressed:

- **Structural Integrity**: Ensuring that the existing structure can support the additional weight of water is crucial. Water weighs approximately 1000 kg/m³, and the added load must be considered in the design.

- **Water Quality**: Existing structures may harbor contaminants. It is vital to assess and remediate any potential sources of pollution before using them for water storage.

- **Accessibility**: The design must allow for easy access to the storage system for maintenance, cleaning, and water extraction.

- **Regulatory Compliance**: Local regulations may dictate how retrofitted structures can be used for water storage, including safety and environmental standards.

Methods of Retrofitting

Several methods can be employed to retrofit existing structures for water storage:

- **Installing Tanks**: Large, food-grade plastic or fiberglass tanks can be installed in basements or garages. These tanks should be equipped with proper inlet and outlet valves, overflow systems, and filtration units.

- **Sealing and Insulating**: To prevent leaks and contamination, existing structures may need to be sealed with waterproof coatings. Insulation may also be necessary to protect against temperature fluctuations.

- **Creating Catchment Systems**: Roofs can be retrofitted with gutters and downspouts that channel rainwater directly into the storage system. This method not only captures rainwater but also reduces runoff.

- **Utilizing Existing Plumbing**: Existing plumbing systems can be modified to divert water into storage tanks. This may include installing valves and pumps to facilitate water movement.

Examples of Successful Retrofitting

Case Study 1: Urban Basement Cistern

In an urban setting, a homeowner retrofitted their basement to include a 5000-liter cistern. The cistern was installed beneath the floor, with a pump system to draw water for irrigation and toilet flushing. The project included sealing the walls with waterproof paint and installing a filtration system to ensure water quality.

Case Study 2: Garage Water Storage

A community center retrofitted an unused garage into a water storage facility by installing multiple 1000-liter tanks. The tanks were connected to the roof's gutter system, allowing rainwater collection. The garage was insulated to prevent freezing during winter, and a filtration system was added to ensure safe water for non-potable uses.

Maintenance and Upkeep

Regular maintenance is essential for the longevity and effectiveness of retrofitted water storage systems:

- **Inspecting Seals and Joints**: Regular checks for leaks and deterioration of seals are critical to maintain water quality and structural integrity.

- **Cleaning Tanks**: Tanks should be cleaned periodically to remove sediment and prevent algae growth. This can be done using a mixture of vinegar and water or specialized tank cleaning solutions.

- **Testing Water Quality**: Routine testing for contaminants is crucial, especially if the water is intended for potable use. Testing kits can be purchased for common contaminants such as bacteria, nitrates, and heavy metals.

Conclusion

Retrofitting existing structures for water storage is a sustainable and efficient approach to enhancing water availability. By understanding the principles of water storage, assessing the suitability of structures, addressing challenges, and implementing effective retrofitting methods, individuals and communities can create reliable water sources that contribute to resilience in the face of water scarcity. This approach not only maximizes the use of existing resources but also promotes environmental stewardship and sustainability.

Rainwater Harvesting Systems

Collecting Rainwater in Underground Tanks

Collecting rainwater in underground tanks is a sustainable method for ensuring a reliable water supply. This section outlines the principles, methods, and considerations involved in effectively harvesting rainwater for storage in underground tanks.

Theoretical Framework

Rainwater harvesting relies on the principle of collecting precipitation from surfaces, such as roofs, and channeling it into storage systems. The amount of rainwater that can be harvested depends on several factors, including the area of the catchment surface, the intensity of rainfall, and the efficiency of the collection system. The volume of rainwater that can be collected can be estimated using the following equation:

$$V = A \times P \times E \tag{33}$$

Where:

- V = Volume of collected rainwater (liters)
- A = Area of the catchment surface (square meters)
- P = Precipitation depth (meters)
- E = Efficiency factor (a decimal representing the efficiency of the collection system, typically between 0.7 and 0.9)

Designing the Collection System

The first step in collecting rainwater is to design an effective collection system. Key components include:

- **Catchment Area:** Typically, roofs are used as catchment surfaces. The material of the roof should be non-toxic and suitable for drinking water.

- **Gutters and Downspouts:** These should be installed to direct rainwater from the roof to the storage tank. Ensure that gutters are clean and free from debris to maximize collection efficiency.

- **First Flush Diverters:** These devices help to divert the initial runoff, which may contain contaminants from the roof, away from the storage tank.

Choosing the Right Underground Tank

When selecting an underground tank for rainwater storage, consider the following factors:

- **Material:** Tanks can be made from various materials such as plastic, concrete, or fiberglass. Each material has its advantages and disadvantages in terms of durability, cost, and installation requirements.

- **Size:** The size of the tank should be determined based on the estimated rainfall in your area, the catchment area, and your water usage needs. A larger tank can provide a more reliable supply, especially in dry seasons.

- **Location:** The tank should be placed in a location that is easily accessible for maintenance and is away from potential contaminants. Additionally, consider the depth of frost lines in colder climates to prevent freezing.

Installation Process

The installation of an underground rainwater tank involves several steps:

1. **Excavation:** Dig a hole that is slightly larger than the tank dimensions to allow for backfill and stabilization.

2. **Base Preparation:** Level the base of the hole and add a layer of sand or gravel for drainage and support.

3. **Tank Placement:** Carefully lower the tank into the hole, ensuring it is level and stable.

4. **Connecting the System:** Connect the downspouts to the tank inlet, ensuring a secure and watertight fit. Install any necessary first flush diverters.

5. **Backfilling:** Once the tank is in place and connected, backfill the excavation with soil, taking care not to damage the tank.

Maintenance and Monitoring

Regular maintenance is crucial for ensuring the efficiency and longevity of your underground rainwater harvesting system. Key maintenance tasks include:

- **Cleaning Gutters and Downspouts:** Regularly inspect and clean gutters to prevent blockages.

- **Tank Inspection:** Periodically check the tank for signs of leaks or structural damage.

- **Water Quality Testing:** Conduct tests on the stored water to check for contaminants, especially if the water is intended for potable use.

Challenges and Solutions

While collecting rainwater in underground tanks is beneficial, several challenges may arise:

- **Contamination:** To mitigate this, install first flush diverters and ensure that the catchment area is clean and free from pollutants.

- **Tank Overflows:** In periods of heavy rainfall, tanks may overflow. Design an overflow system that directs excess water away from the tank and prevents flooding.

- **Regulatory Issues:** Be aware of local regulations regarding rainwater harvesting and ensure compliance by obtaining necessary permits.

Conclusion

Collecting rainwater in underground tanks is a practical solution for enhancing water security. By understanding the theoretical principles, designing an effective collection system, and ensuring proper maintenance, individuals can successfully harness rainwater as a sustainable resource for their needs. This method not only conserves water but also contributes to environmental sustainability.

Sizing Your Rainwater Harvesting System

To effectively design a rainwater harvesting system, it is crucial to accurately size the components to ensure that the system meets your water needs while optimizing efficiency. This section outlines the fundamental principles for sizing your rainwater harvesting system, including calculations for catchment area, storage capacity, and system efficiency.

Understanding Water Demand

Before sizing your rainwater harvesting system, you must first determine your water demand. This involves calculating the daily and seasonal water requirements for your household or intended use. The average daily water consumption per person can vary, but a common estimate is approximately 50-100 liters per day.

$$\text{Total Daily Water Demand} = \text{Number of People} \times \text{Average Daily Consumption} \tag{34}$$

For example, for a family of four with an average consumption of 80 liters per person per day:

$$\text{Total Daily Water Demand} = 4 \times 80 = 320 \text{ liters/day} \tag{35}$$

Estimating Rainfall and Catchment Area

Next, you need to estimate the amount of rainwater you can collect. This is determined by the local average annual rainfall and the size of your catchment area, typically the roof area that will collect rainwater.

The formula for calculating the potential rainwater collection is:

$$\text{Rainwater Harvested} = \text{Catchment Area} \times \text{Annual Rainfall} \times \text{Runoff Coefficient} \tag{36}$$

The runoff coefficient accounts for the efficiency of water collection, which varies depending on the material of the catchment surface. For example, a metal roof has a runoff coefficient of approximately 0.9, while a shingle roof may have a coefficient closer to 0.7.

Assuming a catchment area of 100 m² and an average annual rainfall of 800 mm (0.8 m), the calculation would be:

$$\text{Rainwater Harvested} = 100 \text{ m}^2 \times 0.8 \text{ m} \times 0.9 = 72 \text{ m}^3 \tag{37}$$

This translates to 72,000 liters of rainwater that can potentially be harvested in a year.

RAINWATER HARVESTING SYSTEMS

Calculating Storage Capacity

The next step is to size the storage capacity of your rainwater harvesting system. The storage tank should be large enough to hold sufficient water to meet your needs during dry periods. A common approach is to size your tank to hold at least one month's worth of water demand.

$$\text{Required Storage Capacity} = \text{Total Daily Water Demand} \times \text{Days of Autonomy} \quad (38)$$

For a family of four requiring 320 liters per day and planning for a 30-day autonomy:

$$\text{Required Storage Capacity} = 320 \text{ liters/day} \times 30 \text{ days} = 9,600 \text{ liters} \quad (39)$$

This means you would need a storage tank with a capacity of at least 9,600 liters.

System Efficiency Considerations

When sizing your rainwater harvesting system, consider the efficiency of the system. Factors such as evaporation, leakage, and sedimentation can reduce the amount of usable water. A general rule of thumb is to account for a system efficiency of about 70-80%.

$$\text{Effective Water Supply} = \text{Rainwater Harvested} \times \text{System Efficiency} \quad (40)$$

Using our previous example with 72,000 liters harvested and an efficiency of 75%:

$$\text{Effective Water Supply} = 72,000 \text{ liters} \times 0.75 = 54,000 \text{ liters} \quad (41)$$

This means that, after accounting for inefficiencies, you can expect to have about 54,000 liters of usable water from your rainwater harvesting system annually.

Example Calculation

To summarize the sizing process, consider the following example:

- **Household Size**: 4 people - **Average Daily Consumption**: 80 liters/person - **Catchment Area**: 100 m² - **Annual Rainfall**: 800 mm - **Runoff Coefficient**: 0.9 - **Days of Autonomy**: 30 days

1. Calculate Total Daily Water Demand:

$$\text{Total Daily Water Demand} = 4 \times 80 = 320 \text{ liters/day}$$

2. Calculate Rainwater Harvested:

$$\text{Rainwater Harvested} = 100 \times 0.8 \times 0.9 = 72,000 \text{ liters/year}$$

3. Calculate Required Storage Capacity:

$$\text{Required Storage Capacity} = 320 \times 30 = 9,600 \text{ liters}$$

4. Calculate Effective Water Supply:

$$\text{Effective Water Supply} = 72,000 \times 0.75 = 54,000 \text{ liters}$$

In this example, the system can meet the water demand, with sufficient storage capacity to cover the household's needs during dry periods, assuming the calculations are accurate and local conditions are favorable.

Conclusion

Sizing your rainwater harvesting system correctly is essential for ensuring that it meets your water needs efficiently. By understanding your water demand, estimating rainfall and catchment area, calculating storage capacity, and accounting for system efficiency, you can design a system that is both practical and sustainable. This strategic approach will enable you to harness rainwater effectively, contributing to your overall water security.

Filtering and Treating Rainwater for Safe Consumption

Rainwater harvesting presents a sustainable method for water collection, but ensuring its safety for consumption is paramount. This section will explore various filtering and treatment methods that can be employed to make rainwater safe for human use, focusing on both theoretical underpinnings and practical applications.

RAINWATER HARVESTING SYSTEMS

Understanding Rainwater Contaminants

Rainwater can be contaminated by a variety of sources, including:

- **Atmospheric Pollutants:** Dust, pollen, and pollutants from industrial activities can be collected by raindrops.

- **Roof and Gutter Contaminants:** Materials from roofs (e.g., shingles, metal, or tiles) and debris from gutters can introduce pathogens, heavy metals, and organic matter into the harvested water.

- **Microbial Contaminants:** Bacteria, viruses, and protozoa can thrive in stagnant water and can be introduced through animal droppings or decaying organic matter.

Filtration Methods

To make rainwater safe for consumption, it is essential to first filter out larger particles and contaminants. Several filtration methods can be employed:

1. Sedimentation Sedimentation is a passive method where collected rainwater is allowed to stand for a period, allowing heavier particles to settle at the bottom. The clear water can then be siphoned from the top. While simple, this method is often inadequate for removing smaller pathogens.

2. Mechanical Filtration Mechanical filters, such as screen filters or sand filters, can remove particulate matter effectively.

$$\text{Filtration Efficiency} = \frac{\text{Number of Particles Removed}}{\text{Total Number of Particles}} \times 100\% \qquad (42)$$

For example, a sand filter can remove particles larger than 20 microns, while a finer filter can target smaller particles down to 1 micron.

3. Activated Carbon Filtration Activated carbon filters are effective in removing organic compounds, chlorine, and volatile organic compounds (VOCs). The adsorption process can be described by the following equation:

$$Q_e = \frac{(C_0 - C_e) \cdot V}{m} \qquad (43)$$

Where: - Q_e = Amount of solute adsorbed per unit mass of adsorbent (mg/g) - C_0 = Initial concentration of the solute (mg/L) - C_e = Equilibrium concentration of the solute (mg/L) - V = Volume of solution (L) - m = Mass of adsorbent (g)

This method is particularly useful in urban areas where rainwater may be contaminated with pollutants from vehicles and industrial activities.

Disinfection Methods

After filtration, it is crucial to disinfect the water to eliminate any remaining pathogens. Several methods can be employed:

1. Chemical Disinfection Chlorination is a common method for disinfecting water. The dosage required can be calculated using the following equation:

$$D = \frac{C \cdot V}{T} \tag{44}$$

Where: - D = Dosage of chlorine (mg/L) - C = Desired concentration of free chlorine (mg/L) - V = Volume of water (L) - T = Contact time (minutes)

A typical dosage is 1-3 mg/L of chlorine for effective disinfection, with a contact time of at least 30 minutes.

2. UV Disinfection Ultraviolet (UV) light disinfection is an effective method that requires no chemicals. The effectiveness of UV disinfection can be described by the following equation:

$$D = \frac{I \cdot t}{C} \tag{45}$$

Where: - D = Disinfection efficiency (log reduction) - I = Intensity of UV light (mW/cm²) - t = Time of exposure (seconds) - C = Concentration of pathogens (CFU/mL)

A UV dose of 30 mJ/cm² is typically sufficient for the inactivation of most bacteria and viruses.

3. Solar Disinfection (SODIS) SODIS is a simple method that uses sunlight to purify water. Clear plastic bottles are filled with water and exposed to direct sunlight for at least six hours. The UV radiation and heat work together to kill pathogens.

Storage Considerations

Once rainwater has been filtered and disinfected, proper storage is essential to maintain its quality. Here are some key considerations:

- **Container Material:** Use food-grade plastic or glass containers that are opaque to prevent algae growth.

- **Sealing:** Ensure containers are sealed tightly to prevent contamination from dust, insects, or animals.

- **Location:** Store water in a cool, dark place to minimize degradation and bacterial growth.

Conclusion

Filtering and treating rainwater for safe consumption is a multi-step process that requires careful consideration of contaminants, filtration methods, disinfection techniques, and storage solutions. By employing these methods, individuals can effectively harness rainwater as a reliable and safe water source, contributing to sustainable water management practices.

In summary, the combination of sedimentation, mechanical filtration, activated carbon treatment, and disinfection methods such as chlorination or UV treatment, followed by proper storage, ensures that harvested rainwater is safe for human consumption. Implementing these strategies not only enhances water quality but also promotes self-sufficiency in water management.

Integrating Rainwater Harvesting with Existing Water Systems

Integrating rainwater harvesting (RWH) systems with existing water supply systems can significantly enhance water availability, reduce reliance on municipal sources, and promote sustainability. This integration involves designing a system that allows for the seamless use of harvested rainwater alongside conventional water sources.

Theoretical Framework

The integration of RWH systems with existing water systems can be understood through the concept of a dual supply system. This system combines both harvested rainwater and traditional water supply, allowing users to optimize water usage based on availability, quality, and cost. The theoretical foundation rests on the principles of hydrology, water resource management, and system design.

The key equations governing water flow and storage in such systems include:

$$Q = A \cdot v \qquad (46)$$

where Q is the flow rate (m³/s), A is the cross-sectional area of the flow (m²), and v is the velocity of water (m/s).

Additionally, the storage capacity of rainwater tanks can be calculated using:

$$V = h \cdot A \qquad (47)$$

where V is the volume of water stored (m³), h is the height of water in the tank (m), and A is the base area of the tank (m²).

Challenges in Integration

Integrating RWH systems with existing water systems presents several challenges:

- **Water Quality Management:** Rainwater can be contaminated by pollutants from rooftops and gutters. It is essential to implement filtration and purification systems to ensure that harvested rainwater meets safety standards for potable use.

- **System Compatibility:** Existing plumbing and water distribution systems may require modifications to accommodate the dual supply. This may involve installing additional valves, pumps, and controls to manage the flow between rainwater and municipal sources.

- **Regulatory Compliance:** Local regulations may dictate how rainwater can be harvested and used. It is crucial to consult local authorities to ensure compliance with water rights, health codes, and environmental regulations.

- **Cost Considerations:** Initial investment in RWH systems can be significant. However, the long-term savings on water bills and reduced demand on municipal systems can offset these costs over time.

Practical Implementation Steps

To successfully integrate RWH systems with existing water supply systems, consider the following steps:

1. **System Assessment:** Evaluate your current water supply system, including plumbing, storage, and usage patterns. Identify potential points of integration for rainwater.

2. **Design the RWH System:** Create a design that includes collection surfaces (e.g., roofs), conveyance systems (gutters and downspouts), storage tanks, and distribution systems. Ensure that the design allows for easy switching between rainwater and municipal water sources.

3. **Install Filtration and Treatment:** Incorporate filtration systems to remove debris and contaminants from harvested rainwater. Consider UV treatment or chemical disinfection to ensure water quality.

4. **Connect to Existing Systems:** Work with a qualified plumber to connect the RWH system to your existing water supply. This may involve installing backflow preventers and control valves to manage the flow of water effectively.

5. **Monitor and Maintain:** Regularly inspect and maintain both the RWH and existing water systems. Monitor water quality and usage patterns to optimize the system's performance.

Case Study Example

A practical example of successful integration can be seen in the case of a residential home in a suburban area. The homeowners installed a rainwater harvesting system that collects runoff from their roof, which is then directed into a 5,000-liter underground tank.

The system was designed to automatically switch between rainwater and municipal water supply based on the water level in the tank. When the tank reaches a predetermined low level, the system activates the municipal water supply to ensure a continuous flow of water to the household.

To ensure water quality, the rainwater undergoes a multi-stage filtration process, including a first flush diverter to remove initial contaminants, followed by a sediment filter and UV treatment before entering the household plumbing.

The integration not only reduced the household's water bill by 40% but also contributed to local water conservation efforts by decreasing demand on the municipal supply during dry seasons.

Conclusion

Integrating rainwater harvesting with existing water systems presents a viable solution to enhance water sustainability. By addressing challenges related to water quality, system compatibility, regulatory compliance, and cost, individuals and communities can effectively utilize harvested rainwater, ensuring a resilient and reliable water supply. Through careful planning and implementation, RWH systems can complement existing water infrastructure, promoting conservation and sustainability in water resource management.

Innovative Techniques for Extracting Underground Water

Passive Collection Methods

Capillary Action and Wicking Systems

Capillary action, also known as capillarity, is the ability of a liquid to flow in narrow spaces without the assistance of external forces. This phenomenon occurs due to the interplay of cohesive forces (the attraction between like molecules) and adhesive forces (the attraction between unlike molecules). In survival situations, understanding and harnessing capillary action can provide innovative methods for extracting water from the ground, particularly in arid environments or during times of water scarcity.

Theoretical Background

Capillary action is governed by the principles of fluid mechanics and can be explained using the following equation, which describes the height h to which a liquid will rise in a capillary tube:

$$h = \frac{2\gamma \cos(\theta)}{\rho g r} \tag{48}$$

Where:

- h = height of the liquid column (m)
- γ = surface tension of the liquid (N/m)
- θ = contact angle between the liquid and the surface (degrees)

- ρ = density of the liquid (kg/m³)
- g = acceleration due to gravity (m/s²)
- r = radius of the capillary tube (m)

This equation illustrates that the height to which water can rise in a capillary tube is inversely proportional to the radius of the tube; smaller tubes allow water to rise higher due to the increased effect of adhesive forces.

Practical Applications

In survival scenarios, capillary action can be utilized through the following methods:

Wicking Systems Wicking systems rely on materials that can draw water through capillary action. Common materials include:

- **Cotton Fabric:** Cotton fibers have a high capillarity due to their structure. A simple wicking system can be constructed by burying one end of a cotton strip in moist soil while allowing the other end to hang above ground. Water will be drawn up the strip, providing a steady source of moisture.

- **Bamboo or Hollow Sticks:** These natural materials can act as capillary tubes. By placing one end in water and the other end exposed, water will rise through the bamboo, allowing for collection.

- **Sponge:** A sponge can absorb water through capillary action and can be used to transfer moisture from the ground to a container.

Challenges and Limitations

While capillary action presents various opportunities for water extraction, there are challenges that must be considered:

- **Soil Type:** The effectiveness of capillary action is highly dependent on soil texture. Sandy soils have larger particles and lower capillarity, while clay soils, with their smaller particles, can retain water but may not allow for efficient water movement.

- **Humidity Levels:** In extremely dry conditions, the rate of water absorption may be insufficient to meet needs. Therefore, wicking systems may require supplementary water sources.

- **Material Saturation:** Once the wicking material becomes saturated, its effectiveness decreases. Regular monitoring and replacement of the material may be necessary to maintain efficiency.

Examples of Capillary Action in Nature

Capillary action is not only a theoretical concept but is also observed in nature. For example:

- **Plant Roots:** Plants utilize capillary action to draw water from the soil through their roots, which are designed to maximize surface area and enhance water absorption.
- **Soil Moisture Retention:** In healthy ecosystems, soil microorganisms and organic matter improve the soil structure, enhancing its capillary properties and water retention capabilities.

Conclusion

Harnessing capillary action and wicking systems can be a valuable tool for survivalists seeking to extract water from the ground. By understanding the principles behind capillary action and employing natural materials, individuals can create effective water collection systems. However, it is crucial to consider the limitations imposed by soil type, humidity, and material saturation to optimize these methods in various environmental conditions. Exploring the synergy between nature's designs and human ingenuity can lead to innovative solutions for water scarcity in survival scenarios.

Utilizing Plants as Natural Water Filters

Plants have long been recognized for their ability to filter and purify water, utilizing natural processes that can be harnessed for survival situations. This section explores how plants can serve as effective natural water filters, detailing the underlying theory, potential challenges, and practical examples of their application.

Theoretical Background

The ability of plants to filter water is largely attributed to their root systems, which interact with soil and water in complex ways. This process is often referred to as *phytoremediation*, where plants absorb, degrade, or immobilize contaminants in the soil and water. Key mechanisms involved in this process include:

- **Absorption:** Roots can take up water and dissolved substances, including nutrients and contaminants. This is facilitated by root hairs that increase the surface area for absorption.

- **Filtration:** As water moves through the soil, particulate matter is physically filtered out. The soil matrix traps sediments, pathogens, and other pollutants.

- **Biodegradation:** Certain plants can metabolize harmful substances through biological processes, effectively breaking them down into less harmful compounds.

The effectiveness of plants as water filters can be quantified using the following equation, which estimates the rate of contaminant removal:

$$R = \frac{C_i - C_f}{C_i} \times 100\% \qquad (49)$$

where R is the removal efficiency, C_i is the initial concentration of the contaminant, and C_f is the final concentration after filtration.

Challenges and Limitations

While utilizing plants as natural water filters presents a promising solution, several challenges must be considered:

- **Plant Selection:** Not all plants possess the same filtering capabilities. Species must be carefully selected based on their known effectiveness in removing specific contaminants.

- **Growth Conditions:** The efficiency of plants in filtering water is heavily influenced by environmental conditions such as soil quality, moisture levels, and sunlight.

- **Contaminant Types:** Some contaminants, particularly heavy metals or persistent organic pollutants, may not be effectively removed by plants. Understanding the limitations of phytoremediation is crucial.

- **Time Factor:** The natural filtration process can be slow. In emergency situations, immediate access to clean water may be required, necessitating supplementary filtration methods.

Practical Examples

Implementing plant-based water filtration systems can be achieved through various methods. Below are a few examples:

Constructed Wetlands Constructed wetlands mimic natural wetlands and utilize a variety of wetland plants to filter water. The design typically involves a shallow basin filled with gravel or sand, where water flows through and is treated by the plant roots and associated microorganisms. Common plants used include *Phragmites australis* (common reed) and *Typha* spp. (cattails). These systems are effective for removing nutrients, sediments, and pathogens.

Vegetated Swales Vegetated swales are shallow, landscaped channels designed to manage water runoff. They are planted with grasses and shrubs that filter pollutants while allowing water to percolate into the ground. For instance, using native grasses like *Sorghastrum nutans* (Indiangrass) can enhance the filtration process while supporting local biodiversity.

Biofiltration Systems In urban environments, biofiltration systems can be integrated into stormwater management. These systems utilize a combination of soil, plants, and engineered media to treat runoff. For example, the use of *Juncus effusus* (soft rush) in biofiltration systems has been shown to effectively reduce sediment and nutrient loads.

Conclusion

Utilizing plants as natural water filters offers a sustainable and eco-friendly approach to water purification. By understanding the theoretical mechanisms, addressing challenges, and implementing practical examples, survivalists can effectively harness the power of nature to enhance their water supply. However, careful planning and consideration of local plant species and environmental conditions are essential for successful implementation.

Using Gravity to Your Advantage in Underground Water Collection

Gravity plays a crucial role in the movement and collection of underground water. By understanding and utilizing gravitational forces, we can enhance our water harvesting techniques, ensuring a more reliable and efficient collection system. This section explores the principles of gravity-driven water collection, its practical applications, and the challenges that may arise.

Theoretical Background

Gravity, defined as the force that attracts two bodies towards each other, is a fundamental force that influences the movement of water through soil and rock layers. The gravitational force can be described mathematically by Newton's law of universal gravitation:

$$F = G \frac{m_1 m_2}{r^2} \quad (50)$$

where: - F is the gravitational force between two masses, - G is the gravitational constant (6.674×10^{-11} m^{3}kg^{-1}s^{-2}), - m_1 and m_2 are the masses of the two bodies, - r is the distance between the centers of the two masses.

In the context of underground water collection, we focus on how gravity affects water movement through porous media, such as soil and rock formations. The movement of water through these media is influenced by the principles of hydrostatics and hydrodynamics.

Gravity and Water Flow

When water infiltrates the ground, it moves downward due to gravity. The rate at which water moves through soil is affected by several factors, including soil texture, structure, and moisture content. The Darcy's law, which describes the flow of fluids through porous media, can be expressed as:

$$Q = k \cdot A \cdot \frac{\Delta h}{L} \quad (51)$$

where: - Q is the volumetric flow rate, - k is the hydraulic conductivity of the soil, - A is the cross-sectional area through which the water flows, - Δh is the difference in hydraulic head (height) between two points, - L is the length of the flow path.

By maximizing the difference in hydraulic head (Δh), we can enhance the flow rate of water towards our collection point.

Practical Applications

To utilize gravity effectively in underground water collection, several techniques can be employed:

- **Constructing Trenches and Ditches:** Digging trenches or ditches that slope towards a collection point can guide water flow. By ensuring the trench has a downward gradient, water will naturally flow into the desired area. The slope should be calculated to maintain a balance between water flow and soil erosion.

- **Creating French Drains:** A French drain consists of a perforated pipe surrounded by gravel, placed in a trench that directs water away from a specific area. The perforations allow water to enter the pipe, which uses gravity to transport the water to a designated storage area.

- **Utilizing Natural Topography:** Assessing the natural landscape can reveal low-lying areas where water naturally accumulates. Constructing collection systems in these areas can harness gravity to collect water without extensive excavation.

- **Building Collection Pits:** A collection pit can be dug at a lower elevation than surrounding areas. As water flows through the soil, it will gravitate towards the pit, allowing for efficient harvesting.

Challenges and Solutions

While utilizing gravity for water collection is effective, several challenges may arise:

- **Soil Saturation:** During heavy rainfall, soil can become saturated, leading to runoff instead of infiltration. To mitigate this, consider implementing swales or berms to slow down water flow and encourage infiltration.

- **Erosion:** The movement of water can cause soil erosion, especially on steep slopes. To combat this, use vegetation to stabilize the soil and create barriers that reduce the speed of water flow.

- **Water Quality:** Water collected through gravity may contain contaminants from the soil. Implementing filtration systems at collection points can help purify water before storage.

Examples of Gravity-Driven Water Collection

- **Rainwater Harvesting Systems:** Many rainwater harvesting systems utilize gravity to direct water from rooftops into storage tanks. Gutters and downspouts are strategically placed to ensure efficient collection.

- **Spring Water Collection:** Springs often occur at lower elevations where groundwater emerges. By constructing collection systems at these sites, water can be harvested efficiently using gravity.

- **Agricultural Applications:** Farmers often design fields with contour plowing or terracing to manage water flow effectively. These techniques use gravity to direct water towards crops while minimizing erosion.

In conclusion, harnessing gravity in underground water collection is a powerful technique that can enhance water availability and efficiency. By understanding the principles of gravity and applying practical methods, individuals can significantly improve their water harvesting strategies. As with all survival techniques, careful planning and consideration of local conditions are essential for success.

Harnessing Atmospheric Moisture for Water Extraction

The extraction of atmospheric moisture is a vital technique in regions where traditional water sources are scarce or contaminated. This method capitalizes on the natural humidity present in the air, converting it into usable water through various technologies. Understanding the principles behind atmospheric moisture extraction can empower individuals to develop sustainable water solutions in survival situations.

Theory of Atmospheric Moisture

Atmospheric moisture exists in the form of water vapor, which is the gaseous state of water. The amount of water vapor that air can hold is dependent on temperature and pressure, described by the **Clausius-Clapeyron equation:**

$$\frac{dP}{dT} = \frac{L}{T(V_g - V_l)} \qquad (52)$$

Where: - P is the vapor pressure, - T is the temperature, - L is the latent heat of vaporization, - V_g is the specific volume of the gas, - V_l is the specific volume of the liquid.

This equation illustrates that as temperature increases, the capacity of air to hold moisture also increases, making warmer climates more conducive to moisture extraction.

Methods of Atmospheric Moisture Extraction

There are several innovative techniques for extracting water from the atmosphere, each with its own advantages and limitations. Below, we discuss the most common methods:

1. Dew Harvesting Dew harvesting involves collecting moisture that condenses on surfaces during the night. As temperatures drop, water vapor in the air condenses into liquid water on cooler surfaces, such as metal or plastic sheets.

To optimize dew collection:

- **Surface Material:** Use materials with high thermal conductivity to cool rapidly, such as aluminum.

- **Surface Design:** Create sloped surfaces to facilitate water flow towards a collection point.

- **Location:** Position collection surfaces in areas with high humidity and low wind exposure.

2. Fog Nets Fog nets capture tiny water droplets from fog, which can then coalesce and drip into a collection system. This method is particularly effective in coastal and mountainous regions where fog is prevalent.

Key considerations for fog nets include:

- **Mesh Size:** Use fine mesh to maximize droplet capture while allowing air to flow through.

- **Orientation:** Install nets perpendicular to prevailing winds to maximize exposure.

- **Collection System:** Integrate a gutter system to channel collected water into storage containers.

3. Atmospheric Water Generators (AWGs) AWGs utilize refrigeration techniques to extract moisture from the air. By cooling air below its dew point, water vapor condenses into liquid water, which is then collected and purified.

Important factors for AWGs:

- **Energy Source:** AWGs require a power source; consider solar panels for remote applications.

- **Humidity Levels:** AWGs are most effective in areas with relative humidity above 30%.

- **Maintenance:** Regular cleaning and maintenance are essential to prevent mold and ensure water quality.

Challenges in Atmospheric Moisture Extraction

While atmospheric moisture extraction offers potential solutions for water scarcity, several challenges must be addressed:

1. Efficiency The efficiency of moisture collection methods can vary significantly based on environmental conditions. For instance, dew harvesting is most effective in arid climates during cool nights, while fog nets require specific geographical features.

2. Water Quality Water extracted from the atmosphere may still require purification to ensure safety. Contaminants such as particulate matter, microorganisms, and chemical pollutants can compromise water quality.

3. Resource Availability The practicality of these methods often depends on local resources and climate conditions. For instance, AWGs may not be feasible in regions with limited electricity or high operational costs.

Examples of Atmospheric Moisture Extraction

Several successful implementations of atmospheric moisture extraction techniques illustrate their effectiveness:

1. Dew Harvesting in Namibia In Namibia, communities have successfully implemented dew harvesting systems to provide potable water in arid regions. By using specially designed metal sheets, they collect dew during the night, yielding several liters of water per night.

2. Fog Nets in Chile In the Atacama Desert of Chile, fog nets have been installed to capture moisture from coastal fog. These nets can produce hundreds of liters of water per day, significantly improving water availability for local communities.

ACTIVE EXTRACTION METHODS

3. AWGs in Urban Areas In urban settings, AWGs have been deployed to provide drinking water in areas with limited access to clean water. These systems can be powered by renewable energy sources, making them sustainable alternatives to traditional water supply methods.

Conclusion

Harnessing atmospheric moisture for water extraction is a promising approach to address water scarcity in various environments. By understanding the underlying principles and employing effective techniques, individuals can create sustainable water sources, enhancing their resilience in survival situations. As climate change continues to impact traditional water supplies, these innovative methods will play an increasingly vital role in ensuring access to clean water.

Active Extraction Methods

Pumping and Siphoning Techniques

In survival scenarios, accessing underground water efficiently is crucial. Two effective methods for extracting water from underground sources are pumping and siphoning. Each technique has its own applications, advantages, and limitations, which we will explore in detail.

Pumping Techniques

Pumping involves using a mechanical device to lift water from a lower elevation to a higher one, making it suitable for extracting water from wells, cisterns, or underground aquifers. The fundamental principle of a pump is based on the conversion of mechanical energy into hydraulic energy.

Types of Pumps 1. **Hand Pumps:** These are manually operated pumps that are ideal for small-scale water extraction. Hand pumps can be installed over a well or a cistern and typically consist of a cylinder with a piston. When the handle is pulled up and down, it creates a vacuum that draws water up from the source.

$$P = \frac{F}{A}$$

Where P is the pressure, F is the force applied, and A is the area of the piston. The efficiency of hand pumps can vary, but they are generally reliable for depths up to 20-30 feet.

2. Electric Pumps: For larger-scale extraction, electric pumps can be utilized. These pumps are powered by electricity and can lift water from greater depths. Submersible pumps, for example, are designed to be submerged in water and can pump water to the surface using a motorized impeller.

3. Solar-Powered Pumps: In remote areas where electricity is unavailable, solar-powered pumps offer a sustainable alternative. These pumps harness solar energy to operate, making them ideal for long-term water extraction in off-grid situations.

Challenges with Pumping - **Power Supply:** Electric pumps require a reliable power source. In emergency situations, this can be a significant limitation. - **Maintenance:** Pumps require regular maintenance to ensure they function correctly. Clogged filters or damaged components can hinder water extraction. - **Cost:** Depending on the type of pump, initial costs can be high, especially for electric or solar-powered models.

Siphoning Techniques

Siphoning is a passive method of transferring water from one location to another using gravitational force. This technique relies on the principle of atmospheric pressure and the continuity of fluid flow.

How Siphoning Works To siphon water, a tube is used to create a continuous flow from a higher elevation to a lower one. The basic principle can be described by Bernoulli's equation, which relates the pressure, velocity, and height of the fluid:

$$P + \frac{1}{2}\rho v^2 + \rho g h = \text{constant}$$

Where: - P is the pressure of the fluid, - ρ is the density of the fluid, - v is the velocity of the fluid, - g is the acceleration due to gravity, - h is the height above a reference point.

When the tube is filled with water and one end is placed in the lower container, the gravitational force acting on the water column creates a pressure difference that allows water to flow from the higher source to the lower destination.

Steps for Siphoning 1. **Fill the Tube:** Submerge the entire tube in the water source to fill it completely, eliminating air bubbles. 2. **Create a Vacuum:** Cover one end of the tube with your thumb and quickly move it to the lower container. 3.

ACTIVE EXTRACTION METHODS 99

Release and Flow: Once the tube is positioned, release your thumb. The water will flow due to gravitational pull.

Advantages of Siphoning - **Simplicity:** Siphoning requires minimal equipment and can be performed with basic tubing. - **No Power Needed:** This method does not require any mechanical power, making it ideal for emergency situations.

Limitations of Siphoning - **Elevation Difference:** Siphoning only works if there is a sufficient height difference between the water source and the destination. If the source is not elevated, siphoning will not be effective. - **Contamination Risk:** Care must be taken to ensure the tube does not introduce contaminants into the water supply.

Practical Applications and Examples

1. **Hand Pump Example:** In a survival situation, a hand pump can be installed over a shallow well. By regularly operating the pump, a household can access clean water without relying on external power sources.
2. **Siphoning Example:** If a rainwater collection barrel is situated on a higher platform than a garden, a siphon can be used to transfer water to the plants without the need for pumps or electricity.

In conclusion, both pumping and siphoning techniques offer valuable methods for extracting underground water. Understanding the principles, applications, and limitations of each method allows individuals to make informed decisions in survival situations where water access is critical.

Hand-Operated Water Extraction Tools

In survival situations, having access to water is crucial, and hand-operated water extraction tools can be invaluable for retrieving water from underground sources. These tools are particularly beneficial in areas where electricity is unavailable or where solar-powered systems may not be feasible. This section explores various hand-operated water extraction tools, their principles of operation, and practical examples of their use.

Types of Hand-Operated Water Extraction Tools

Several types of hand-operated tools can be employed to extract water from underground sources. The most common include:

- Hand Pumps
- Siphons
- Bailers
- Water Witches

Hand Pumps

Hand pumps are mechanical devices that allow users to extract water from wells or underground aquifers. They typically consist of a cylinder, piston, and handle. The operation of a hand pump is based on the principles of atmospheric pressure and suction.

$$P = \frac{F}{A} \tag{53}$$

Where:

- P is the pressure,
- F is the force applied,
- A is the area of the piston.

When the handle is pulled up, the piston creates a vacuum that draws water into the cylinder. As the handle is pushed down, the water is forced out through a spout. Hand pumps can vary in design, including:

- **Pitcher Pumps:** These are simple pumps that can be used for shallow wells (up to 25 feet deep).
- **Deep Well Pumps:** Designed for deeper sources, these pumps often require more effort to operate.

Siphons

Siphoning is a technique that utilizes gravity to move water from one location to another without the need for a pump. The basic principle of siphoning can be described as follows:

$$h_1 - h_2 = \frac{2g}{g} \cdot \Delta P \tag{54}$$

Where:

ACTIVE EXTRACTION METHODS

- h_1 is the height of the water source,
- h_2 is the height of the discharge point,
- g is the acceleration due to gravity,
- ΔP is the pressure difference.

To create a siphon, one must fill a flexible tube with water, ensuring no air bubbles are trapped. The tube is then placed with one end in the water source and the other end at a lower elevation. Once the water begins to flow, it will continue until the water levels equalize or the siphon is disrupted.

Bailers

Bailers are simple, cylindrical containers used to collect water from wells or other underground sources. They can be made from various materials, including plastic or metal, and are operated manually. The operation of a bailer is straightforward:

$$V = \pi r^2 h \tag{55}$$

Where:

- V is the volume of water collected,
- r is the radius of the bailer,
- h is the height of the water column.

To use a bailer, the user lowers it into the water source, allowing it to fill. Once full, the bailer is pulled back up, and the water can be poured out. Bailers are effective for shallow wells and can be easily constructed from available materials.

Water Witches

Water witching, or dowsing, is a traditional method of locating underground water sources using a forked stick or metal rods. While the scientific validity of water witching is debated, many practitioners claim success in finding water. The principle behind water witching involves the belief that the dowser can sense vibrations or energy changes when over a water source.

Practical Considerations

When selecting a hand-operated water extraction tool, consider the following:

- **Depth of Water Source:** Determine how deep the water source is to choose an appropriate tool. Hand pumps are suitable for deeper sources, while bailers and siphons work well for shallow ones.

- **Water Quality:** Always assess the quality of the water extracted. Contaminated water can pose health risks, so purification methods should follow extraction.

- **Maintenance:** Regularly inspect and maintain tools to ensure they function correctly and safely.

Conclusion

Hand-operated water extraction tools provide essential methods for accessing underground water sources in survival situations. Understanding the principles of operation and application of these tools can significantly enhance one's ability to secure clean water. By utilizing hand pumps, siphons, bailers, and even traditional methods like water witching, individuals can effectively manage their water needs in various environments. Always remember to prioritize water quality and safety in any extraction process.

Solar-Powered Water Extraction Systems

Solar-powered water extraction systems harness the abundant energy of the sun to extract water from underground sources, making them an efficient and sustainable solution for water scarcity. These systems can be particularly beneficial in remote areas where traditional power sources are unavailable or unreliable.

Theory Behind Solar-Powered Extraction

Solar-powered water extraction systems typically rely on photovoltaic (PV) cells to convert sunlight into electricity, which then powers water pumps or other extraction mechanisms. The fundamental equation governing the efficiency of solar panels is given by:

$$P = \eta \cdot A \cdot G \tag{56}$$

where:

ACTIVE EXTRACTION METHODS

- P is the electrical power output (in watts),
- η is the efficiency of the solar panel (a percentage),
- A is the area of the solar panel (in square meters),
- G is the solar irradiance (in watts per square meter).

This equation illustrates that the power output of a solar panel is directly proportional to its efficiency and the amount of sunlight it receives, as well as its surface area.

Components of Solar-Powered Extraction Systems

A typical solar-powered water extraction system consists of the following components:

- **Solar Panels:** Convert sunlight into electrical energy.
- **Inverter:** Converts direct current (DC) generated by solar panels into alternating current (AC) for use by water pumps.
- **Water Pump:** Extracts water from underground sources using the power generated by the solar panels.
- **Storage Tank:** Stores extracted water for later use.
- **Control System:** Monitors and regulates the operation of the system to optimize performance.

Advantages of Solar-Powered Systems

The benefits of using solar-powered water extraction systems include:

- **Sustainability:** Utilizing solar energy reduces dependence on fossil fuels and minimizes carbon emissions.
- **Cost-Effectiveness:** After the initial investment, operational costs are low as sunlight is free and abundant.
- **Low Maintenance:** Solar panels require minimal maintenance, and many pumps are designed for durability.
- **Remote Accessibility:** These systems can be deployed in remote areas where grid electricity is unavailable.

Challenges and Considerations

While solar-powered water extraction systems offer numerous advantages, they also face certain challenges:

- **Initial Costs:** The upfront investment for solar panels and pumps can be significant.

- **Weather Dependency:** The efficiency of the system can be affected by weather conditions, such as cloudy days and seasonal variations in sunlight.

- **Storage Solutions:** Adequate water storage must be planned to account for periods of low sunlight.

Practical Example: Solar-Powered Well Pumping

Consider a scenario in a rural area where a community relies on a solar-powered well pumping system. The system is designed with a 1 kW solar panel array, an inverter, and a submersible pump capable of delivering 2,000 liters per day.

Assuming an average solar irradiance of 5 hours/day (which is a common value in many sunny regions), the daily energy produced by the solar panels can be calculated as:

$$E = P \cdot t = 1000 \, \text{W} \cdot 5 \, \text{h} = 5000 \, \text{Wh} = 5 \, \text{kWh} \tag{57}$$

If the pump operates at an efficiency of 70%, the effective energy available for pumping water is:

$$E_{\text{effective}} = E \cdot \eta = 5000 \, \text{Wh} \cdot 0.7 = 3500 \, \text{Wh} \tag{58}$$

Assuming the pump requires 0.5 kWh to extract 1,000 liters of water, the total volume of water that can be extracted daily is:

$$V = \frac{E_{\text{effective}}}{\text{Energy per liter}} = \frac{3500 \, \text{Wh}}{0.5 \, \text{kWh}} = 7000 \, \text{liters} \tag{59}$$

This example illustrates how solar-powered systems can provide a reliable source of water in areas where it is needed most.

Conclusion

Solar-powered water extraction systems represent a viable and sustainable solution for addressing water scarcity issues. By leveraging renewable energy, these systems not only enhance water accessibility but also contribute to environmental conservation. As technology continues to advance, the efficiency and affordability of these systems are expected to improve, making them an increasingly attractive option for communities worldwide.

Using Hydraulic Pressure for Water Extraction

Hydraulic pressure refers to the force exerted by a fluid in a confined space, which can be harnessed for various applications, including water extraction from underground sources. This method is particularly useful when dealing with deep water tables or when traditional methods of extraction, such as hand digging or pumping, are impractical.

Theory of Hydraulic Pressure

The fundamental principle behind hydraulic pressure is described by Pascal's Law, which states that a change in pressure applied to an enclosed fluid is transmitted undiminished to all portions of the fluid and the walls of its container. Mathematically, this can be expressed as:

$$P = \frac{F}{A} \tag{60}$$

where:

- P is the pressure (in Pascals, Pa),
- F is the force applied (in Newtons, N),
- A is the area over which the force is applied (in square meters, m^2).

When utilizing hydraulic systems for water extraction, the pressure generated can be used to lift water from underground sources through pipes or tubes.

Designing a Hydraulic Extraction System

A basic hydraulic extraction system consists of the following components:

- **Pump**: A device that creates a vacuum or pressure to draw water from underground.
- **Piping**: Tubes that transport water from the source to the storage area.
- **Reservoir**: A storage unit for the extracted water.

Calculating Required Pressure

To determine the necessary hydraulic pressure for extracting water from a certain depth, the hydrostatic pressure formula can be applied:

$$P = \rho g h \tag{61}$$

where:

- ρ is the density of water (approximately 1000 kg/m^3),
- g is the acceleration due to gravity (9.81 m/s^2),
- h is the depth of the water source (in meters).

For example, if the water table is located at a depth of 10 m, the required pressure to extract water can be calculated as follows:

$$P = 1000 \text{ kg/m}^3 \times 9.81 \text{ m/s}^2 \times 10 \text{ m} = 98100 \text{ Pa or } 98.1 \text{ kPa} \tag{62}$$

This pressure must be generated by the pump to effectively extract water from that depth.

Common Problems in Hydraulic Extraction

While hydraulic pressure systems can be effective, they are not without challenges:

- **Air Leaks**: Any leaks in the system can lead to a loss of pressure, rendering the extraction ineffective.
- **Pump Failure**: Mechanical failure of the pump can halt the extraction process, necessitating regular maintenance.
- **Clogging**: Sediment and debris can clog pipes, reducing flow rates and efficiency.

Examples of Hydraulic Extraction Systems

1. **Submersible Pumps**: These are electric pumps that are submerged in the water source. They use hydraulic pressure to push water to the surface. They are commonly used in wells and can efficiently extract water from significant depths.

2. **Hydraulic Ram Pumps**: These devices utilize the energy of falling water to lift a portion of that water to a height. They are particularly useful in areas with flowing streams and can operate without external power.

3. **Hand Pumps**: Simple hand-operated pumps can be designed to use hydraulic pressure principles, allowing individuals to extract water manually. These are suitable for shallow wells or when electricity is unavailable.

Conclusion

Using hydraulic pressure for water extraction is a powerful method that can provide access to underground water sources effectively. By understanding the principles of hydraulic pressure, designing appropriate systems, and addressing common challenges, individuals can harness this technique to ensure a reliable water supply in survival situations.

Purifying and Storing Underground Water

Techniques for Water Purification

Filtration Systems for Removing Sediments and Particles

Filtration is a crucial process in water purification, particularly for removing sediments and particles that may compromise water quality. This section will explore various filtration systems, their underlying principles, common problems associated with sediment filtration, and practical examples of their application.

Understanding Filtration

Filtration is a physical separation process that removes solid particles from liquids or gases by using a porous medium. The fundamental principle of filtration is based on size exclusion, where particles larger than the pores of the filter medium are trapped, while water passes through.

The effectiveness of a filtration system can be described by the following equation:

$$Q = \frac{A \cdot \Delta P}{\mu} \qquad (63)$$

Where:

- Q is the flow rate of water through the filter (m³/s),

- A is the cross-sectional area of the filter (m²),

- ΔP is the pressure difference across the filter (Pa),

- μ is the viscosity of the fluid (Pa·s).

This equation illustrates that the flow rate is directly proportional to the pressure difference and the area of the filter, while inversely proportional to the viscosity of the fluid.

Types of Filtration Systems

Various filtration systems can be employed to remove sediments and particles from water. The choice of filtration system depends on the specific application, the type of contaminants present, and the desired water quality.

1. Sand Filters   Sand filters are one of the most common types of filtration systems used for sediment removal. They consist of layers of sand and gravel, which trap larger particles as water flows through. The effectiveness of sand filters is influenced by the size of the sand grains and the depth of the filter bed.

- **Advantages:** Low cost, easy maintenance, and effective for removing suspended solids.
- **Disadvantages:** Limited effectiveness for smaller particles and requires regular backwashing to maintain flow rates.

2. Cartridge Filters   Cartridge filters utilize a replaceable filter element made of various materials, such as pleated polyester or cellulose, to capture sediments and particles. They are often used in household water filtration systems.

- **Advantages:** Compact design, high filtration efficiency, and ease of replacement.
- **Disadvantages:** Higher operational costs due to the need for frequent replacements and limited capacity for large volumes of water.

3. Membrane Filters   Membrane filtration systems use semi-permeable membranes to separate particles from water. These systems can achieve very high levels of purification, capable of removing bacteria, viruses, and even dissolved solids.

- **Advantages:** High filtration efficiency and effectiveness against microorganisms.

TECHNIQUES FOR WATER PURIFICATION

- **Disadvantages:** Higher initial costs, potential for membrane fouling, and the need for regular maintenance.

Common Problems in Filtration

While filtration systems are effective at removing sediments and particles, several challenges can arise during their operation:

1. Clogging Clogging occurs when particles accumulate on the filter medium, reducing flow rates and increasing pressure differentials. This can lead to inefficient filtration and may require more frequent maintenance.

To mitigate clogging, it is essential to pre-treat water to remove larger debris before it enters the filtration system. Regular monitoring and maintenance schedules can also help maintain optimal flow rates.

2. Filter Breakthrough Filter breakthrough happens when the filter becomes saturated and can no longer retain particles, allowing them to pass through the system. This can compromise water quality and pose health risks if pathogens are present.

To prevent filter breakthrough, operators should monitor the pressure drop across the filter and replace or clean the filter media as needed. Implementing a multi-stage filtration approach can also enhance overall efficiency.

3. Chemical Contaminants While filtration systems are effective for removing physical particles, they may not adequately address chemical contaminants. This limitation necessitates the use of additional treatment methods, such as activated carbon filtration or reverse osmosis, to ensure comprehensive water purification.

Practical Examples

Example 1: Sand Filter Installation In a rural community facing issues with sediment-laden surface water, a sand filter system was installed to improve water quality. The system consisted of a series of sand beds, with the following specifications:

- **Filter Depth:** 1.5 meters
- **Sand Grain Size:** 0.5 to 1.0 mm
- **Flow Rate:** Designed to handle 10 m^3/day

The installation resulted in a significant reduction in turbidity levels, improving the overall quality of drinking water.

Example 2: Household Cartridge Filter System A family living in an urban area installed a cartridge filter system to ensure safe drinking water. The system used a pleated filter cartridge with a nominal rating of 5 microns, effectively removing sediments, rust, and other particulates from the water supply.

The family reported improved taste and clarity in their drinking water, highlighting the effectiveness of cartridge filters for residential applications.

Conclusion

Filtration systems are essential for removing sediments and particles from water, ensuring safe and clean drinking water. Understanding the different types of filtration systems, their advantages and limitations, and common problems can help individuals and communities make informed decisions about water purification methods. By implementing effective filtration strategies, it is possible to enhance water quality and safeguard public health.

Chemical Treatments for Disinfection

Chemical disinfection is a crucial step in ensuring the safety of harvested underground water. It involves the use of various chemical agents to eliminate pathogens, including bacteria, viruses, and protozoa, that may pose health risks upon consumption. This section will discuss the theory behind chemical disinfection, common chemical agents used, their application methods, and the challenges associated with their use.

Theory of Chemical Disinfection

Chemical disinfection works by introducing substances that can destroy or inactivate harmful microorganisms. The effectiveness of a chemical disinfectant is influenced by several factors, including concentration, contact time, temperature, and the presence of organic matter. The general principle can be summarized in the following equation:

$$\text{Efficacy} = f(C, t, T, OM) \tag{64}$$

Where: - C = Concentration of the disinfectant - t = Contact time - T = Temperature of the solution - OM = Presence of organic matter

TECHNIQUES FOR WATER PURIFICATION

Higher concentrations and longer contact times generally increase efficacy, but the presence of organic matter can shield microorganisms from chemical agents, reducing their effectiveness.

Common Chemical Agents for Disinfection

Several chemical agents are widely used for disinfecting water. Each has its advantages and disadvantages, as outlined below:

- **Chlorine:**
    - *Mechanism:* Chlorine reacts with water to form hypochlorous acid ($HOCl$), which is a strong oxidizing agent that can destroy pathogens.
    - *Application:* Typically used in a gas or liquid form. The recommended dosage is 1-5 mg/L for disinfection, depending on water quality.
    - *Limitations:* Chlorine can react with organic matter to form disinfection byproducts (DBPs), some of which are harmful.

- **Chloramine:**
    - *Mechanism:* Chloramine is formed by combining chlorine with ammonia, providing a longer-lasting disinfectant effect than chlorine alone.
    - *Application:* Used in concentrations of 2-4 mg/L. It is particularly effective in systems with high organic content.
    - *Limitations:* Less effective against certain pathogens compared to chlorine and may require longer contact times.

- **Ozone:**
    - *Mechanism:* Ozone (O_3) is a powerful oxidant that can destroy pathogens by breaking down their cellular structures.
    - *Application:* Typically generated on-site and used in concentrations of 0.5-2 mg/L. Ozone must be applied with care due to its instability.
    - *Limitations:* Ozone has a short half-life and must be used immediately. It also requires post-treatment deactivation as it can be harmful to human health.

- **Hydrogen Peroxide:**

- *Mechanism:* Hydrogen peroxide (H_2O_2) acts as an oxidizing agent, producing free radicals that can damage microbial cells.
- *Application:* Used in concentrations of 1-5 mg/L. It is effective against a broad spectrum of pathogens.
- *Limitations:* Requires careful handling and can be unstable if not stored correctly.

Application Methods

The application of chemical disinfectants can be performed using several methods, including:

- **Batch Treatment:** Involves adding the disinfectant to a specific volume of water in a controlled environment and allowing it to mix thoroughly for the required contact time before use.
- **Continuous Disinfection:** Involves the continuous addition of disinfectant to a water supply, ensuring that the water remains disinfected as it flows through the system.
- **Residual Disinfection:** Ensures that a certain level of disinfectant remains in the water after treatment to provide ongoing protection against recontamination during storage and distribution.

Challenges and Considerations

While chemical disinfection is effective, it is not without challenges:

- **Formation of Disinfection Byproducts (DBPs):** The reaction of disinfectants with organic matter can lead to the formation of DBPs, some of which are toxic. Regular monitoring and adjustment of disinfectant levels are essential to minimize this risk.
- **Resistance of Microorganisms:** Some pathogens, particularly protozoa like Cryptosporidium, are resistant to certain chemical treatments. Alternative or additional disinfection methods may be required for effective removal.
- **Chemical Storage and Handling:** Many disinfectants are hazardous materials that require careful storage and handling to prevent accidents and ensure safety.

- **Regulatory Compliance:** Users must be aware of and comply with local regulations regarding the use of chemical disinfectants, including allowable concentrations and monitoring requirements.

Conclusion

Chemical treatments for disinfection are vital for ensuring the safety of underground water sources. By understanding the mechanisms, applications, and challenges associated with various chemical agents, individuals can effectively implement disinfection strategies that safeguard their water supply. Regular monitoring and adherence to safety protocols are essential to maximize the benefits of chemical disinfection while minimizing potential risks.

UV and Solar Disinfection Methods

Ultraviolet (UV) disinfection and solar disinfection are effective methods for purifying water, particularly in survival situations where access to advanced treatment facilities is limited. Both methods harness the power of UV radiation to inactivate pathogens, making water safe for consumption.

Understanding UV Disinfection

UV disinfection involves exposing water to UV light, which is a part of the electromagnetic spectrum. The wavelengths typically used for disinfection range from 200 to 300 nanometers, with the most effective wavelength being around 254 nanometers. At this wavelength, UV light penetrates the cells of microorganisms, damaging their DNA or RNA and rendering them unable to reproduce and cause infection.

The effectiveness of UV disinfection can be quantified using the following equation:

$$D = \frac{E}{C} \qquad (65)$$

where:

- D is the disinfection dose (mJ/cm^2),
- E is the energy of UV light (mW/cm^2),
- C is the flow rate of water (cm/s).

A higher disinfection dose correlates with a greater reduction in pathogen levels. Research indicates that a UV dose of at least 30 mJ/cm^2 is required to achieve a 99.9% reduction of common pathogens, including E. coli and Giardia.

Advantages of UV Disinfection

- **Chemical-Free:** UV disinfection does not require the addition of chemicals, making it environmentally friendly.
- **Rapid Action:** The process is instantaneous, providing immediate results.
- **Broad Spectrum:** UV light is effective against a wide range of microorganisms, including bacteria, viruses, and protozoa.

Limitations of UV Disinfection

Despite its advantages, UV disinfection has limitations:

- **Water Clarity:** UV effectiveness is significantly reduced in turbid water. Suspended solids can shield microorganisms from UV light.
- **No Residual Protection:** Unlike chemical treatments, UV does not provide residual disinfection, meaning that water can become re-contaminated after treatment.
- **Power Requirement:** UV systems require electricity, which may not be available in emergency situations.

Solar Disinfection (SODIS)

Solar disinfection, or SODIS, is a simple and cost-effective method of purifying water using sunlight. This technique is particularly useful in regions with abundant sunlight and limited resources. The process involves filling clear plastic bottles with contaminated water and exposing them to direct sunlight for a specified duration, typically six hours or more.

The effectiveness of SODIS can be attributed to two primary mechanisms:

- **UV Radiation:** Similar to UV disinfection, the UV rays from the sun inactivate pathogens.
- **Heat:** The temperature increase from solar radiation can further enhance the disinfection process, as many pathogens are sensitive to heat.

SODIS Guidelines

To effectively utilize SODIS, follow these guidelines:

- Use only clear, transparent plastic bottles, as colored or opaque containers will reduce UV penetration.

- Ensure the bottles are clean and free from scratches, as scratches can harbor microorganisms.

- Place the bottles in direct sunlight, ideally on a reflective surface to maximize exposure.

- Monitor the weather; cloudy days may reduce effectiveness, requiring longer exposure times.

Limitations of SODIS

While SODIS is an excellent method for water disinfection, it has its limitations:

- **Time-Consuming:** SODIS requires several hours of direct sunlight, which may not be feasible in all situations.

- **Dependence on Weather:** Cloudy or rainy conditions can significantly hinder the effectiveness of this method.

- **Not Suitable for All Contaminants:** SODIS is effective against many pathogens but may not eliminate all chemical contaminants or heavy metals.

Conclusion

Both UV and solar disinfection methods are vital tools in the arsenal of survival water purification techniques. Understanding their principles, advantages, and limitations allows individuals to make informed decisions in emergency situations. By employing these methods correctly, one can significantly reduce the risk of waterborne diseases, ensuring access to safe drinking water in challenging environments.

Electrochemical and Membrane Technologies for Water Purification

Water purification is critical in ensuring safe drinking water, particularly when relying on underground sources that may be contaminated. Two advanced methods of purification—electrochemical and membrane technologies—offer effective solutions for treating water. This section explores the principles, applications, and challenges associated with these techniques.

Electrochemical Water Purification

Electrochemical water purification involves the use of electrical energy to drive chemical reactions that remove contaminants from water. This method can effectively eliminate bacteria, viruses, heavy metals, and organic pollutants. The primary processes include electrocoagulation, electrooxidation, and electroflotation.

Electrocoagulation Electrocoagulation (EC) employs an electric current to destabilize and aggregate suspended particles and colloids in water. The process can be described by the following reaction:

$$M^{n+} + e^- \to M \tag{66}$$

where M^{n+} represents metal ions (e.g., aluminum or iron) that, upon reduction, form metal hydroxides that trap contaminants.

Electrooxidation Electrooxidation utilizes anodes to generate oxidants such as chlorine or ozone, which can effectively degrade organic pollutants. The general reaction at the anode can be represented as follows:

$$2Cl^- \to Cl_2 + 2e^- \tag{67}$$

Chlorine can react with organic compounds to form non-toxic byproducts, thus purifying the water.

Electroflotation Electroflotation combines electrocoagulation and flotation processes. Microbubbles generated at the anode attach to contaminants, causing them to rise to the surface for easy removal. The efficiency of this process can be influenced by several factors, including current density and water chemistry.

Challenges of Electrochemical Purification

While electrochemical methods are effective, they face several challenges:

- **Energy Consumption:** High energy requirements can limit the feasibility of these systems in remote areas.
- **Electrode Fouling:** Accumulation of contaminants on electrodes can decrease efficiency and increase maintenance needs.
- **Chemical Byproducts:** The formation of harmful byproducts during electrochemical reactions must be managed to prevent secondary pollution.

Membrane Technologies for Water Purification

Membrane filtration is a widely used method in water treatment, utilizing semi-permeable membranes to separate contaminants from water. The main types of membrane processes include microfiltration, ultrafiltration, nanofiltration, and reverse osmosis.

Microfiltration and Ultrafiltration Microfiltration (MF) and ultrafiltration (UF) membranes operate at different pore sizes, with MF typically removing particles larger than 0.1 micrometers, while UF can remove smaller particles, including bacteria and some viruses.

$$\text{Flux} = \frac{Q}{A \cdot \Delta P} \tag{68}$$

where Q is the flow rate, A is the membrane area, and ΔP is the transmembrane pressure difference.

Nanofiltration and Reverse Osmosis Nanofiltration (NF) membranes can remove divalent ions and small organic molecules, while reverse osmosis (RO) membranes can eliminate nearly all contaminants, including monovalent ions. The driving force for RO is osmosis, and the process can be modeled by the following equation:

$$\Delta \Pi = \Delta P - \Delta \Pi_m \tag{69}$$

where $\Delta \Pi$ is the osmotic pressure difference, ΔP is the applied pressure, and $\Delta \Pi_m$ is the osmotic pressure of the feed solution.

Challenges of Membrane Technologies

Despite their effectiveness, membrane technologies face significant challenges:

- **Membrane Fouling:** Accumulation of particles and organic matter on the membrane surface can reduce efficiency and increase operational costs.
- **Selective Permeability:** Not all membranes are capable of selectively removing specific contaminants, which may require pre-treatment of water.
- **Cost:** The initial investment and maintenance costs for membrane systems can be high, making them less accessible in low-resource settings.

Conclusion

Electrochemical and membrane technologies represent advanced methods for purifying water from underground sources. While both methods offer effective solutions for removing contaminants, they also come with challenges that must be addressed to ensure their successful implementation. Understanding these technologies and their limitations is essential for developing sustainable water purification systems that can be adapted to various environmental conditions and resource availability.

By integrating these advanced purification techniques into water harvesting and storage systems, individuals and communities can enhance their resilience against water scarcity and contamination, ensuring access to safe drinking water in survival situations.

Long-Term Water Storage Solutions

Choosing the Right Containers for Water Storage

When it comes to storing water, the choice of container is crucial for ensuring the water remains safe, clean, and usable over time. The right container will not only preserve the quality of the water but also prevent contamination and degradation. This section will explore the factors to consider when selecting water storage containers, the types of containers available, and best practices for their use.

Factors to Consider

- **Material:** The material of the container plays a significant role in its suitability for water storage. Common materials include:

- **Plastic:** Food-grade polyethylene or polypropylene containers are generally safe for water storage. They are lightweight, durable, and resistant to corrosion. However, they can leach chemicals over time, especially when exposed to sunlight or high temperatures.
  - **Glass:** Glass containers are non-reactive and do not leach chemicals, making them an excellent choice for long-term storage. However, they are heavier and more fragile than plastic.
  - **Metal:** Stainless steel and aluminum are also viable options. Stainless steel is durable and resistant to corrosion, while aluminum may require a food-safe lining to prevent reactions with water.

- **Size and Capacity:** The size of the container should be determined by the intended use and available space. Smaller containers (5 to 20 liters) are easier to handle and can be used for daily needs, while larger tanks (200 liters and above) are suitable for long-term storage. The volume of water needed can be estimated using the following equation:

$$V = N \times D \qquad (70)$$

where V is the total volume of water needed (liters), N is the number of people, and D is the daily water requirement per person (liters).

- **Sealability:** Containers should have tight-fitting lids to prevent contamination from dust, insects, and other pollutants. Airtight seals also help minimize evaporation and maintain water quality.

- **UV Resistance:** If the container will be stored outdoors, it should be UV-resistant to prevent degradation from sunlight exposure. Containers that are opaque or dark in color help block sunlight and reduce algae growth.

- **Portability:** Consider how the container will be transported, especially in emergency situations. Containers with handles or those that are stackable can make transportation and storage easier.

Types of Containers

- **Water Barrels:** Typically made from food-grade plastic or metal, these barrels can store large quantities of water (up to 200 liters). They are ideal for long-term storage and can be used in conjunction with rainwater harvesting systems.

- **Water Jugs:** Smaller than barrels, these jugs (often 5 to 20 liters) are suitable for everyday use and can be easily transported. They are often made from plastic and are available in both opaque and transparent varieties.

- **Cisterns:** These large underground or above-ground tanks can store thousands of liters of water. Cisterns are often made from reinforced concrete, plastic, or fiberglass and are used for rainwater collection and storage.

- **Portable Water Containers:** Collapsible water containers made from durable plastic are excellent for emergency situations. They can be folded when empty, saving space, and are easy to carry.

Best Practices for Water Storage

To ensure the longevity and safety of stored water, follow these best practices:

- **Clean Containers:** Before filling any container with water, it should be thoroughly cleaned and sanitized. Use a solution of unscented household bleach (1 tablespoon per gallon of water) to disinfect the container, followed by rinsing with clean water.

- **Fill to Capacity:** When filling containers, fill them to the top to minimize the air space, which can promote the growth of bacteria and algae.

- **Store in a Cool, Dark Place:** Keep containers in a cool, dark environment to prevent heat and light exposure, which can degrade the container material and promote algae growth.

- **Regularly Rotate Supplies:** Water should be rotated every six months to ensure freshness. Label containers with the date of filling to keep track of their age.

- **Monitor for Contamination:** Periodically check stored water for signs of contamination, such as cloudiness, unusual odors, or floating particles. If contamination is suspected, purify the water before use.

Conclusion

Choosing the right containers for water storage is essential for maintaining water quality and ensuring safe access during emergencies or daily use. By considering factors such as material, size, sealability, and UV resistance, individuals can make informed decisions that enhance their water storage capabilities. Implementing best practices will further ensure that stored water remains safe and usable for extended periods, providing a reliable resource in times of need.

Preventing Contamination and Algae Growth

Maintaining the purity of stored water is crucial for ensuring its safety for consumption. Contamination can occur through various pathways, including physical, chemical, and biological means. Algae growth, in particular, poses a significant risk, as it can lead to the production of toxins and unpleasant tastes and odors. This section outlines effective strategies for preventing contamination and algae growth in water storage systems.

Understanding Contamination Sources

Water contamination can originate from several sources, which can be categorized as follows:

- **Physical Contaminants:** These include sediments, debris, and particulate matter that can enter the water during collection or storage. For example, dust and leaves can accumulate in open storage tanks.

- **Chemical Contaminants:** Chemicals can leach into water from storage materials or external sources, such as pesticides and fertilizers. For instance, using non-food-grade containers can introduce harmful substances into the water.

- **Biological Contaminants:** Microorganisms, including bacteria, viruses, and algae, can proliferate in stored water, particularly if conditions are favorable for their growth.

Preventative Measures

To effectively prevent contamination and algae growth, the following strategies should be implemented:

1. **Choosing Appropriate Storage Containers** The selection of storage containers plays a pivotal role in preventing contamination. Containers should be made of food-grade materials that do not leach harmful chemicals into the water. Common materials include:

- **High-Density Polyethylene (HDPE):** This plastic is widely used for water storage due to its durability and resistance to UV light.

- **Glass Containers:** Glass is inert and does not leach chemicals, making it an excellent choice for small-scale water storage.

- **Stainless Steel Tanks:** These are ideal for larger systems, as they are resistant to rust and corrosion.

2. Sealing and Covering Storage Systems To minimize the risk of contamination, all storage systems should be securely sealed. This can be achieved by:

- Using tight-fitting lids on tanks and containers to prevent debris and animals from entering.

- Installing screens or filters on openings to block insects and larger contaminants.

3. Regular Cleaning and Maintenance Routine cleaning of storage containers is essential to prevent algae and other biological growth. Recommended practices include:

- **Periodic Cleaning:** Empty and scrub storage tanks with a mixture of water and vinegar or a mild bleach solution (1 part bleach to 10 parts water) at least twice a year.

- **Inspection:** Regularly check for signs of algae growth, sediment buildup, or leaks and address issues promptly.

4. Managing Light Exposure Algae thrive in light, particularly sunlight. To inhibit their growth, consider the following:

- **Opaque Containers:** Use dark or opaque containers that block light penetration.

- **Shading:** If possible, place storage tanks in shaded areas or cover them with tarps to reduce light exposure.

5. Water Treatment Techniques   Implementing water treatment techniques can further enhance the quality of stored water and inhibit algae growth:

- **Chlorination:** Adding chlorine can effectively disinfect water and prevent biological growth. The recommended dosage is approximately 2-4 mg/L of chlorine, depending on the water quality.

- **Ultraviolet (UV) Treatment:** UV light can be used to disinfect water, killing bacteria and preventing algae proliferation without introducing chemicals.

Monitoring Water Quality

Regular monitoring of water quality is vital for early detection of contamination. Key parameters to test include:

- **pH Levels:** Algae typically thrive in water with a pH between 6.5 and 8.5. Maintaining a slightly acidic pH can inhibit growth.

- **Turbidity:** High turbidity levels can indicate contamination. Water should be clear, with turbidity levels below 1 NTU (Nephelometric Turbidity Units).

- **Microbial Testing:** Periodically test for the presence of coliform bacteria and other pathogens using water testing kits.

Case Study: Algae Control in Rainwater Harvesting Systems

A community in a semi-arid region implemented a rainwater harvesting system to supplement their water supply. They faced significant challenges with algae growth in their storage tanks. To address this, they took the following measures:

- They constructed the tanks using HDPE materials and painted them dark to minimize light penetration.

- They installed fine mesh screens on all inlet and outlet points to prevent debris and insects from entering the system.

- The community adopted a routine cleaning schedule, emptying the tanks every six months and scrubbing them with a vinegar solution.

- They introduced a UV purification system at the outlet of the storage tanks, ensuring that any remaining microorganisms were eliminated before distribution.

As a result of these interventions, the community successfully reduced algae growth and improved the overall quality of their stored water.

Conclusion

Preventing contamination and algae growth in water storage systems is essential for ensuring safe drinking water. By selecting appropriate containers, sealing systems, maintaining cleanliness, managing light exposure, and employing effective water treatment techniques, individuals can significantly reduce the risk of contamination. Regular monitoring of water quality further enhances safety, ensuring that stored water remains a reliable resource for consumption.

Rotating and Maintaining Stored Water Supplies

In any survival situation, maintaining the quality and usability of stored water supplies is critical. This section discusses the importance of regularly rotating stored water, the methods for doing so, and the maintenance practices that ensure water remains safe for consumption.

Importance of Water Rotation

Water, even when stored in ideal conditions, can degrade over time due to various factors such as container material, exposure to light, and temperature fluctuations. The primary reasons for rotating stored water supplies include:

- **Degradation of Quality:** Over time, even sealed water can develop off-flavors and odors due to the leaching of chemicals from the container or the growth of microorganisms.

- **Preventing Contamination:** Regular rotation helps ensure that any potential contaminants are identified and addressed before they compromise the entire supply.

- **Ensuring Freshness:** Fresh water is vital for hydration, cooking, and hygiene. Rotating supplies guarantees that you have access to the freshest possible water.

Methods for Rotating Water Supplies

To effectively rotate your water supply, consider implementing the following strategies:

1. **Establish a Rotation Schedule** It is recommended to rotate stored water every six months to one year, depending on the storage conditions. Mark containers with the date of filling, and create a calendar reminder to check and rotate supplies.

2. **Use the First In, First Out (FIFO) Method** When adding new water to your storage, always use the FIFO method. This means using the oldest water first, ensuring that you consume the water that has been stored the longest before it degrades.

3. **Monitor Water Levels** Regularly check the water levels in your storage containers. This practice not only helps with rotation but also allows you to identify any leaks or evaporation issues.

Maintaining Water Quality

In addition to rotating your water supply, several maintenance practices can help ensure the quality of your stored water:

1. **Choose Appropriate Containers** Using food-grade plastic or glass containers specifically designed for water storage is essential. Avoid using containers that previously held chemicals or non-food substances, as they may leach harmful substances into the water.

2. **Store in a Cool, Dark Place** Heat and light can accelerate the degradation of stored water. Ideally, water should be stored in a cool, dark place, away from direct sunlight and heat sources. The optimal storage temperature is between 50°F (10°C) and 70°F (21°C).

3. **Seal Containers Properly** Ensure that all containers are tightly sealed to prevent contamination from dust, insects, and other environmental factors. Check seals regularly for any signs of wear or damage.

4. **Test Water Quality Regularly** To ensure that stored water remains safe for consumption, test water quality periodically. Use home water testing kits to check for contaminants such as bacteria, nitrates, and pH levels. If any issues are detected, replace the water immediately.

Example Scenario

Consider a family of four that has a water storage system comprising four 5-gallon containers. They fill these containers with municipal water and store them in a cool basement. To implement a rotation strategy, they label each container with the date of filling:

- Container A: Filled on January 1, 2023
- Container B: Filled on February 1, 2023
- Container C: Filled on March 1, 2023
- Container D: Filled on April 1, 2023

In this scenario, the family decides to rotate their water supply every six months. By July 1, 2023, they will consume Container A first, refilling it with fresh water. They will then continue to rotate the remaining containers in the same manner, ensuring that they always have access to fresh water.

Conclusion

Rotating and maintaining stored water supplies is essential for ensuring access to safe and potable water in emergency situations. By establishing a regular rotation schedule, utilizing the FIFO method, and adhering to proper maintenance practices, individuals and families can effectively manage their water resources. Regular testing and monitoring further enhance the safety and quality of stored water, preparing them for any unforeseen circumstances.

Using Underground Aquifers for Natural Water Storage

Underground aquifers serve as vital reservoirs for natural water storage, providing a sustainable and often reliable source of fresh water. These geological formations can store significant quantities of water, which can be tapped into during periods of scarcity or drought. Understanding the characteristics, challenges, and management of aquifers is essential for effective water resource planning.

Understanding Aquifers

Aquifers are typically composed of porous rock or sediment that can hold and transmit water. They can be classified into two main types:

- **Unconfined Aquifers:** These aquifers are directly recharged by surface water and are not capped by a layer of impermeable rock. The water table in unconfined aquifers fluctuates based on precipitation and evaporation.

- **Confined Aquifers:** These are sandwiched between layers of impermeable rock, which can create pressure within the aquifer. Water in confined aquifers is often under pressure, leading to artesian wells where water can flow to the surface without pumping.

The storage capacity of an aquifer can be described using the following equation:

$$S = V/A \tag{71}$$

where S is the storage capacity (in cubic meters), V is the volume of water stored (in cubic meters), and A is the area of the aquifer (in square meters).

Challenges in Using Aquifers

Despite their benefits, utilizing underground aquifers for natural water storage presents several challenges:

- **Over-extraction:** Excessive withdrawal of water can lead to a decline in the water table, resulting in reduced water availability and potential land subsidence.

- **Contamination:** Aquifers can be vulnerable to pollutants from agricultural runoff, industrial discharges, and septic systems. Contaminated aquifers can pose serious health risks.

- **Recharge Rates:** The rate at which an aquifer can be recharged is dependent on factors such as rainfall, soil permeability, and land use. Over-extraction can exceed the natural recharge capacity, leading to depletion.

Examples of Aquifer Utilization

Several regions around the world exemplify successful management and utilization of aquifers for natural water storage:

- **The Ogallala Aquifer, USA:** This vast aquifer underlies eight states in the Great Plains and serves as a crucial water source for agriculture. However, it is experiencing significant depletion due to heavy irrigation practices.

Sustainable management practices, such as improved irrigation techniques and crop selection, are being implemented to mitigate over-extraction.

- **The Great Artesian Basin, Australia:** This confined aquifer system is one of the largest in the world and provides water for both urban and agricultural use. The basin is managed through strict regulations on water extraction and promotes the use of water-efficient practices in agriculture.

- **The Nubian Sandstone Aquifer System, North Africa:** This transboundary aquifer spans several countries and is crucial for water supply in arid regions. Collaborative management strategies among nations have been initiated to ensure sustainable use and protection against contamination.

Management Strategies for Aquifer Storage

To effectively utilize underground aquifers for natural water storage, the following management strategies should be considered:

- **Monitoring Water Levels:** Regular monitoring of water levels in aquifers can help assess the sustainability of water extraction practices. This can be achieved through the use of piezometers and water level loggers.

- **Recharge Enhancement Techniques:** Techniques such as artificial recharge, where surface water is directed into aquifers, can help restore water levels. This can be done through methods like infiltration basins and recharge wells.

- **Water Conservation Practices:** Implementing water conservation measures in agriculture and urban settings can reduce the demand on aquifers. Practices such as rainwater harvesting and xeriscaping can significantly decrease reliance on groundwater.

- **Public Awareness and Education:** Engaging the community in understanding the importance of aquifers and promoting responsible water use can lead to better management practices and conservation efforts.

Conclusion

Using underground aquifers for natural water storage is a sustainable approach to managing water resources, particularly in areas prone to drought and water scarcity. By understanding the characteristics of aquifers, addressing the challenges they face, and implementing effective management strategies, communities can ensure a reliable supply of fresh water for future generations. Through collaborative efforts and innovative practices, the potential of aquifers can be harnessed to meet the growing demands for water in a changing climate.

Safety Considerations and Regulations

Understanding Water Quality and Testing

Common Contaminants and their Health Risks

In any survival situation, the quality of water is paramount. Contaminated water can lead to a host of health issues, making it essential to understand common water contaminants and their associated risks. This section discusses various contaminants, their sources, potential health effects, and strategies for mitigation.

Microbial Contaminants

Microbial contaminants include bacteria, viruses, and protozoa that can cause waterborne diseases. Common pathogens include:

- **Escherichia coli (E. coli):** This bacterium is often found in fecal matter and can cause severe gastrointestinal distress. Symptoms include diarrhea, abdominal cramps, and vomiting. In severe cases, it can lead to hemolytic uremic syndrome (HUS), a life-threatening condition.

- **Giardia lamblia:** A protozoan parasite that causes giardiasis, characterized by symptoms such as diarrhea, fatigue, and weight loss. Giardia is often present in water contaminated by animal feces.

- **Cryptosporidium:** Another protozoan that causes cryptosporidiosis, leading to severe diarrhea and dehydration. It is resistant to many common water treatment methods.

- **Norovirus:** A highly contagious virus that can cause gastroenteritis. It is often transmitted through contaminated water, leading to outbreaks, especially in crowded places.

Chemical Contaminants

Chemical contaminants can originate from agricultural runoff, industrial discharges, and household waste. Key chemical contaminants include:

- **Heavy Metals:** Metals such as lead, mercury, and arsenic can leach into water sources from industrial processes and old plumbing. Lead exposure can cause developmental issues in children and cardiovascular problems in adults. Arsenic is a known carcinogen linked to skin, bladder, and lung cancer.

- **Pesticides and Herbicides:** Chemicals used in agriculture can contaminate nearby water sources. Prolonged exposure to certain pesticides has been linked to neurological disorders and hormonal disruptions.

- **Nitrates and Nitrites:** Commonly found in fertilizers, high levels of nitrates can cause methemoglobinemia, or "blue baby syndrome," in infants, which affects the ability of blood to carry oxygen.

- **Volatile Organic Compounds (VOCs):** These compounds can evaporate into the air and contaminate water supplies, often from industrial activities. Exposure can lead to liver damage, respiratory issues, and increased cancer risk.

Physical Contaminants

Physical contaminants include sediments and turbidity, which can affect water quality and clarity. While not always harmful in themselves, they can harbor pathogens and interfere with disinfection processes.

- **Sediments:** Soil and organic matter can enter water supplies through erosion and runoff. High sediment levels can reduce water quality and hinder filtration and disinfection efforts.

- **Turbidity:** This refers to the cloudiness of water caused by suspended particles. Turbid water can indicate the presence of pathogens and can reduce the effectiveness of disinfection methods such as UV treatment.

Health Risks Associated with Contaminants

The health risks associated with water contaminants can vary widely based on the type of contaminant, exposure levels, and individual susceptibility. Key health risks include:

- **Gastrointestinal Illnesses:** Many microbial contaminants lead to gastrointestinal diseases, which can result in dehydration, malnutrition, and even death in severe cases, particularly among vulnerable populations such as children and the elderly.

- **Neurological Disorders:** Long-term exposure to heavy metals and certain pesticides can result in cognitive impairments, developmental delays in children, and increased risk of neurodegenerative diseases.

- **Cancer:** Chemical contaminants like arsenic and certain VOCs are classified as carcinogens, increasing the risk of various cancers with prolonged exposure.

- **Reproductive and Developmental Issues:** Some contaminants, particularly heavy metals and pesticides, can disrupt endocrine functions, leading to reproductive issues, birth defects, and developmental delays in children.

Mitigation Strategies

To protect against the health risks associated with contaminated water, several strategies can be employed:

- **Water Testing:** Regular testing for microbial and chemical contaminants can help identify potential issues before they pose health risks. Home testing kits are available for various contaminants.

- **Filtration and Purification:** Using appropriate filtration systems, such as activated carbon filters, reverse osmosis units, or UV purifiers, can effectively reduce or eliminate many contaminants.

- **Boiling Water:** Boiling water for at least one minute (or three minutes at higher altitudes) can kill most pathogens, making it a reliable method for purifying water in emergency situations.

- **Source Protection:** Protecting water sources from contamination through proper waste disposal, maintaining buffer zones around water bodies, and using sustainable agricultural practices can help ensure water quality.

Understanding common water contaminants and their health risks is crucial for effective water management in survival situations. By employing appropriate testing and purification methods, individuals can safeguard their health and ensure access to safe drinking water.

Methods for Testing Water Quality

Testing water quality is crucial to ensure its safety for consumption and use. Various methods can be employed to assess water quality, each with its advantages and limitations. Understanding these methods can help individuals select the most appropriate technique based on their specific circumstances.

Physical Testing Methods

Physical testing involves assessing the physical characteristics of water, such as color, turbidity, and temperature. These parameters can provide immediate insights into the water's quality.

1. **Color and Turbidity** Color can indicate the presence of dissolved organic matter or contaminants. Turbidity, measured in Nephelometric Turbidity Units (NTU), indicates the clarity of water. High turbidity can harbor pathogens and reduce the efficacy of disinfection methods.

$$\text{Turbidity (NTU)} = \frac{I}{I_0} \times 100 \qquad (72)$$

where I is the intensity of scattered light and I_0 is the intensity of incident light.

2. **Temperature** Water temperature affects chemical reactions and biological activity. It is essential to measure temperature using a calibrated thermometer, as temperature fluctuations can impact water quality.

Chemical Testing Methods

Chemical testing provides a more in-depth analysis of water quality by identifying specific contaminants and their concentrations.

1. **pH Testing** The pH level indicates the acidity or alkalinity of water, influencing the solubility of metals and the availability of nutrients. A pH meter or pH test strips can be used for this purpose.

$$\text{pH} = -\log_{10}[\text{H}^+] \tag{73}$$

where [H$^+$] is the concentration of hydrogen ions in moles per liter.

2. Dissolved Oxygen (DO) Dissolved oxygen is vital for aquatic life. Low levels can indicate pollution or excessive organic matter. The Winkler method or a DO meter can be used to measure dissolved oxygen levels.

3. Chemical Contaminants Testing for specific chemical contaminants such as nitrates, phosphates, heavy metals, and pesticides is essential. Test kits are available for various contaminants, allowing for field testing.

Biological Testing Methods

Biological testing assesses the presence of microorganisms in water, which can pose health risks.

1. Total Coliform Testing Total coliform bacteria are indicators of potential contamination. A positive test suggests the presence of harmful pathogens. The membrane filtration method is commonly used for this purpose.

2. E. coli Testing Testing for E. coli specifically indicates fecal contamination and potential health risks. The IDEXX Colilert method provides a rapid assessment of E. coli levels.

Advanced Analytical Techniques

For comprehensive water quality assessment, advanced analytical techniques may be employed.

1. Gas Chromatography-Mass Spectrometry (GC-MS) GC-MS is used to detect and quantify organic compounds in water. It provides detailed information on pollutants and is commonly used in laboratory settings.

2. Atomic Absorption Spectroscopy (AAS) AAS is used to determine the concentration of metals in water samples. It is highly sensitive and can detect trace levels of heavy metals.

Field Testing Kits

Field testing kits offer a practical solution for on-site water quality testing. These kits typically include test strips, reagents, and instructions for measuring key parameters such as pH, turbidity, and the presence of specific contaminants. While convenient, the accuracy of field kits can vary, and they may not provide comprehensive results.

Conclusion

Choosing the appropriate method for testing water quality depends on the specific contaminants of concern, available resources, and the required level of accuracy. Regular testing and monitoring are essential to ensure water safety and to take corrective actions when necessary. Understanding the various methods of testing empowers individuals to make informed decisions regarding their water sources and to safeguard their health and well-being.

Interpreting Water Test Results

Interpreting water test results is a crucial step in ensuring the safety and quality of water sourced from underground reserves. Understanding the implications of various contaminants, their concentrations, and the standards set by health organizations will guide effective decision-making regarding water purification and usage.

Understanding Water Quality Parameters

Water quality tests typically measure various parameters, including:

- **Physical Characteristics:** These include color, turbidity, odor, and temperature. For instance, turbidity (cloudiness) can indicate the presence of suspended particles, which may harbor pathogens.

- **Chemical Contaminants:** These can be divided into organic and inorganic substances. Common tests include pH, total dissolved solids (TDS), heavy metals (like lead and arsenic), nitrates, and phosphates.

- **Biological Contaminants:** This includes the presence of bacteria, viruses, and protozoa. Tests often focus on coliform bacteria, which serve as indicators of fecal contamination.

Interpreting Numerical Results

Each parameter is typically reported in specific units. Understanding these units is crucial for interpretation:

- **pH:** A pH scale ranges from 0 to 14, with 7 being neutral. Values below 7 indicate acidity, while values above 7 indicate alkalinity. Drinking water should ideally have a pH between 6.5 and 8.5.
- **TDS:** Total dissolved solids are measured in milligrams per liter (mg/L). Water with TDS levels above 500 mg/L may taste salty or bitter and could indicate the presence of harmful contaminants.
- **Coliform Bacteria:** Measured in colony-forming units (CFU) per 100 mL, the presence of E. coli or fecal coliforms indicates potential health risks. A result of 0 CFU/100 mL is the standard for safe drinking water.

Comparing Results to Standards

Water quality standards are established by organizations such as the Environmental Protection Agency (EPA) in the United States. It is essential to compare your test results against these benchmarks:

- **Primary Standards:** These are legally enforceable limits on contaminants that pose health risks. For instance, the maximum contaminant level (MCL) for lead is 0.015 mg/L.
- **Secondary Standards:** These are non-enforceable guidelines regarding aesthetic qualities of water, such as taste and odor. For example, the secondary standard for iron is 0.3 mg/L to prevent staining.

Identifying Problems and Potential Solutions

Upon analyzing the test results, various scenarios may arise:

- **Exceeding MCLs:** If any contaminant exceeds the MCL, immediate action is necessary. For example, if nitrate levels exceed 10 mg/L, it may cause methemoglobinemia, or "blue baby syndrome," in infants. Solutions may include advanced filtration systems or alternative water sources.
- **Aesthetic Issues:** If secondary standards are not met (e.g., high TDS), the water may be safe but unpalatable. Solutions can include carbon filtration or reverse osmosis systems to improve taste and odor.

- **Biological Contamination:** The presence of coliform bacteria indicates a significant health risk. Boiling water or using UV treatment systems can effectively eliminate pathogens.

Example Interpretation

Consider a hypothetical water test result:

- pH: 6.2
- TDS: 600 mg/L
- Nitrates: 12 mg/L
- Coliform: 5 CFU/100 mL

Analysis:

- The pH of 6.2 is slightly acidic and may require adjustment to meet the ideal range.
- TDS at 600 mg/L exceeds the recommended level and may affect taste. Consider filtration options.
- Nitrate levels exceed the safe limit of 10 mg/L, posing health risks, particularly for infants. Investigate the source of contamination and consider treatment options.
- The presence of coliform bacteria indicates fecal contamination. This is a serious concern, necessitating immediate action such as boiling or advanced filtration.

Conclusion

Interpreting water test results is essential for assessing the safety and quality of underground water sources. By understanding the significance of various parameters, comparing them to established standards, and identifying potential problems, individuals can take informed actions to ensure safe drinking water. Regular testing and monitoring are vital components of effective water management strategies, especially in survival situations where access to clean water is critical.

Monitoring and Maintaining Water Quality

Monitoring and maintaining water quality is crucial for ensuring the safety and usability of underground water sources. Contaminated water can pose serious health risks, leading to diseases such as cholera, dysentery, and other waterborne illnesses. This section outlines the key aspects of monitoring water quality, including the identification of contaminants, testing methods, and maintenance strategies.

Understanding Contaminants

Water quality can be compromised by various contaminants, which can be broadly categorized into physical, chemical, and biological contaminants:

- **Physical Contaminants:** These include sediments, turbidity, and color. High turbidity can reduce light penetration, affecting aquatic life and indicating the presence of harmful pathogens.

- **Chemical Contaminants:** These can include heavy metals (e.g., lead, arsenic), pesticides, nitrates, and industrial chemicals. The presence of these substances can arise from agricultural runoff, industrial discharges, or leaching from landfills.

- **Biological Contaminants:** Bacteria, viruses, and protozoa fall under this category. Common pathogens include *Escherichia coli*, *Giardia*, and *Cryptosporidium*, which can cause severe gastrointestinal illnesses.

Methods for Testing Water Quality

Regular testing is essential to monitor water quality effectively. Various methods can be employed:

1. **Field Testing Kits:** Portable kits allow for on-site testing of key parameters such as pH, turbidity, and the presence of specific contaminants. These kits often include colorimetric tests, where the water sample is treated with reagents, and a color change indicates the concentration of a contaminant.

2. **Laboratory Analysis:** For more comprehensive testing, samples can be sent to accredited laboratories. These analyses can detect a broader range of contaminants, including heavy metals and microbial pathogens. The laboratory will often use methods such as Atomic Absorption Spectroscopy (AAS) or Polymerase Chain Reaction (PCR) for precise measurements.

3. **Continuous Monitoring Systems:** In situations where water quality may fluctuate rapidly, continuous monitoring systems can be installed. These systems utilize sensors to measure parameters like turbidity, dissolved oxygen, and conductivity in real-time, providing immediate feedback on water quality.

Interpreting Water Test Results

Once testing is completed, it is vital to interpret the results accurately. Water quality standards, such as those set by the Environmental Protection Agency (EPA) or World Health Organization (WHO), provide guidelines on acceptable contaminant levels. For instance, the EPA has established a Maximum Contaminant Level (MCL) for lead at 0.015 mg/L.

The interpretation process involves comparing test results against these standards. If levels exceed the MCL, immediate action is required to mitigate health risks. For example, if *E. coli* is detected in a drinking water source, it indicates fecal contamination, necessitating immediate disinfection and further investigation into the contamination source.

Monitoring Frequency

The frequency of monitoring depends on several factors, including:

- **Source Type:** Groundwater sources may require less frequent testing compared to surface water, which is more susceptible to contamination from runoff.

- **Usage:** Water sources used for drinking should be tested more frequently than those used for irrigation or industrial purposes.

- **Historical Data:** If previous tests have indicated issues with specific contaminants, more frequent monitoring may be warranted.

A general guideline is to test drinking water sources at least once a year, while more vulnerable sources may require quarterly testing.

Maintaining Water Quality

To ensure ongoing water quality, several maintenance strategies should be implemented:

1. **Regular System Inspections:** Conduct routine inspections of water collection and storage systems to identify potential contamination sources. Look for signs of leaks, corrosion, or biofilm buildup in tanks and pipes.

2. **Proper Filtration and Treatment:** Utilize appropriate filtration systems to remove sediments and pathogens. For instance, a multi-barrier approach that combines sediment filtration, UV disinfection, and activated carbon treatment can effectively improve water safety.

3. **Protecting Source Areas:** Implement land use management practices to protect water source areas from pollution. This includes establishing buffer zones around wells and springs and controlling runoff from agricultural activities.

4. **Educating Users:** Inform all users of the water system about the importance of water quality and encourage practices that minimize contamination risks, such as proper waste disposal and chemical usage.

Conclusion

Monitoring and maintaining water quality is a continuous process that requires diligence and proactive measures. By understanding potential contaminants, utilizing effective testing methods, and implementing maintenance strategies, individuals and communities can ensure the safety and sustainability of their water sources. Regular monitoring not only protects public health but also fosters a deeper connection to the natural water systems that sustain us.

Bibliography

[1] United States Environmental Protection Agency. (n.d.). *Water Quality Standards*. Retrieved from https://www.epa.gov/wqs-tech/water-quality-standards

[2] World Health Organization. (2017). *Guidelines for Drinking-water Quality*. Retrieved from https://www.who.int/publications/i/item/9789241549950

[3] Harris, D. C. (2015). *Quantitative Chemical Analysis*. New York: W.H. Freeman and Company.

[4] Mullis, K., & Faloona, F. (1987). Specific synthesis of DNA in vitro via a polymerase-catalyzed chain reaction. *Methods in Enzymology*, 155, 335-350.

Permitting and Legal Considerations

Regulations for Water Rights and Access

Understanding the regulations surrounding water rights and access is crucial for anyone involved in harvesting and utilizing underground water sources. Water rights are legal entitlements that allow individuals or entities to use water from a specific source, and these rights vary significantly by jurisdiction. This section outlines the fundamental principles governing water rights, common issues faced, and examples of regulations that may apply.

Legal Framework of Water Rights

Water rights can be categorized into two primary systems: the **riparian rights** system and the **prior appropriation** system.

Riparian Rights Riparian rights are typically found in eastern states of the United States and are based on the principle that landowners whose property is adjacent to a water source have the right to use that water. The key aspects of riparian rights include:

- **Reasonable Use:** Landowners can use water as long as it does not adversely affect other riparian users.

- **Natural Flow:** Users must allow water to flow naturally downstream, maintaining its quality and quantity.

Prior Appropriation The prior appropriation system is prevalent in western states, where water is scarce. This system is based on the principle of "first in time, first in right." Key characteristics include:

- **Priority Date:** The first person to use a specific water source has the right to continue using it, regardless of land ownership.

- **Beneficial Use:** Water must be put to beneficial use, such as irrigation, domestic use, or industrial applications.

Common Issues and Challenges

Navigating water rights can be complex, and several challenges may arise:

Conflicts Over Water Use As demand for water increases, conflicts can arise between users, particularly in times of drought. For example, a farmer relying on a river may find their access restricted due to a new industrial user upstream.

Environmental Regulations Many regions have regulations aimed at protecting ecosystems. For instance, the Clean Water Act in the United States imposes restrictions on water withdrawals that may harm aquatic habitats.

Changing Legal Landscapes Water rights laws can evolve, influenced by climate change, population growth, and legal challenges. For example, recent court rulings may redefine water rights in response to environmental concerns, impacting existing users.

Examples of Water Rights Regulations

California Water Rights System In California, the State Water Resources Control Board oversees water rights. Users must apply for permits to divert water, with priority given to those who can demonstrate beneficial use. The system also includes regulations for groundwater extraction, requiring permits for significant withdrawals.

Texas Groundwater Rights Texas operates under a rule of capture for groundwater, allowing landowners to extract unlimited amounts of water from their land. However, this can lead to over-extraction and depletion of aquifers, prompting discussions about implementing more sustainable regulations.

Colorado Doctrine Colorado employs the prior appropriation doctrine, where water rights are quantified based on historical use. Users must file for a water right with the state, including proof of beneficial use, which can be a lengthy process.

Conclusion

Understanding the regulations surrounding water rights and access is essential for sustainable water management. Individuals seeking to harvest underground water must familiarize themselves with local laws, obtain necessary permits, and ensure compliance with environmental regulations. Failure to do so can result in legal disputes, fines, and depletion of vital water resources. Therefore, consulting with legal experts and local authorities is highly recommended to navigate the complexities of water rights effectively.

$$\text{Water Rights} = \text{Legal Entitlement} + \text{Beneficial Use} + \text{Compliance with Regulations} \tag{74}$$

Obtaining Permits for Water Extraction and Storage

In many regions, the extraction and storage of water are subject to various legal regulations. Understanding these regulations is crucial for ensuring that your water harvesting practices are compliant with local laws. This section will outline the steps involved in obtaining the necessary permits for water extraction and storage, as well as the potential issues you may face.

Understanding Local Regulations

Water rights are governed by a complex web of local, state, and federal laws. The first step in obtaining permits is to familiarize yourself with the specific regulations that apply to your area. These regulations can vary significantly depending on the jurisdiction, and they may cover aspects such as:

- The quantity of water you are allowed to extract.
- The methods you can use for extraction.
- The seasons or periods during which extraction is permitted.
- The requirements for water storage, including the type of containers and their locations.

To find this information, consult your local government's water resources department or equivalent agency. Many jurisdictions have online resources that outline the permitting process and provide access to necessary forms and guidelines.

Types of Permits

There are generally two types of permits you may need to obtain for water extraction and storage:

1. **Water Extraction Permits**: These permits are required for the legal withdrawal of water from natural sources, such as rivers, lakes, or underground aquifers. The application process typically involves:
    - Submitting a detailed proposal outlining your intended use of the water.
    - Providing evidence of your water rights, if applicable.
    - Demonstrating that your extraction will not negatively impact the local ecosystem or water availability for other users.

2. **Water Storage Permits**: If you plan to store water, especially in large quantities, you may need a separate permit. The requirements for these permits can include:
    - Specifications on the type and size of storage containers.
    - Safety measures to prevent contamination and overflow.
    - Regular inspections and maintenance protocols.

The Application Process

The application process for obtaining water extraction and storage permits can be lengthy and may involve several steps:

1. **Pre-Application Consultation**: Before submitting an application, it is advisable to consult with local water authorities. This can help clarify any uncertainties regarding the permitting process and requirements.

2. **Filling Out the Application**: Complete the necessary forms, ensuring that all required information is provided. This may include:

   - Your personal details and contact information.
   - A description of the proposed water use.
   - Maps or diagrams of the intended extraction and storage sites.

3. **Submitting Supporting Documents**: Along with your application, you may need to submit additional documentation, such as:

   - Environmental impact assessments.
   - Evidence of ownership or rights to the land where extraction will occur.
   - Technical specifications for extraction and storage systems.

4. **Review Period**: After submission, your application will enter a review period during which local authorities will assess its compliance with regulations. This process can take several weeks or even months, depending on the jurisdiction.

5. **Public Notice and Hearing**: In some cases, particularly for larger projects, a public notice may be required, and a hearing could be held to address any concerns from the community or other stakeholders.

6. **Permit Approval or Denial**: Once the review is complete, you will receive notification of whether your permit has been approved or denied. If denied, you may have the option to appeal the decision or modify your application and reapply.

Common Challenges in Obtaining Permits

Obtaining permits for water extraction and storage can present several challenges, including:

- **Compliance with Environmental Regulations**: Many jurisdictions have stringent environmental regulations aimed at protecting ecosystems and water quality. You may need to conduct thorough assessments and implement mitigation strategies to address potential impacts.
- **Competition for Water Resources**: In areas where water is scarce, competition for water rights can be intense. You may face opposition from other users or stakeholders, which can complicate the permitting process.
- **Changing Regulations**: Water laws and regulations can change over time, sometimes rapidly. Staying informed about any changes that may affect your permits is essential to maintaining compliance.

Examples of Water Extraction and Storage Permits

To illustrate the permitting process, consider the following hypothetical examples:

- **Example 1**: A rural homeowner wishes to install a rainwater harvesting system that includes a large underground cistern. They consult with their local water authority, complete the necessary application forms, and provide a detailed plan for the system. After a review period, they receive approval, but with conditions requiring regular water quality testing.
- **Example 2**: A farmer seeks to extract water from a nearby river for irrigation. They submit an application outlining their intended use and demonstrate that their extraction will not harm local wildlife. However, due to competing claims from other agricultural users, their application is delayed, requiring additional negotiations and adjustments.

Conclusion

Obtaining permits for water extraction and storage is a critical step in ensuring that your practices are legal and sustainable. By understanding local regulations, navigating the application process, and addressing common challenges, you can successfully secure the necessary permissions to harvest and store water responsibly. Always stay informed about local laws and engage with water authorities to facilitate a smooth permitting experience.

Complying with Local Health and Environmental Regulations

When it comes to harvesting and utilizing underground water sources, compliance with local health and environmental regulations is not only a legal obligation but also a critical component of responsible water management. This section will delve into the various aspects of these regulations, the potential problems associated with non-compliance, and provide actionable examples to ensure that your water harvesting practices are both safe and legal.

Understanding Local Regulations

Local regulations regarding water rights and access can vary significantly based on geographic location, state laws, and even municipal codes. It is essential to familiarize yourself with the following aspects:

- **Water Rights:** In many regions, water rights are governed by the principle of "first in time, first in right," meaning that the first user to divert water from a source has the right to continue using it. Understanding your rights in relation to existing water users is crucial.

- **Permitting:** Some jurisdictions require permits for the extraction and use of groundwater, particularly if it involves significant quantities. Permits may also be necessary for the construction of wells or other water collection systems.

- **Environmental Impact Assessments (EIA):** In some cases, an EIA may be required to evaluate the potential environmental impacts of your water harvesting activities. This is particularly relevant for larger projects that may affect local ecosystems.

Potential Problems with Non-Compliance

Failing to comply with local health and environmental regulations can lead to several serious issues, including:

- **Fines and Penalties:** Violations of water use regulations can result in hefty fines, which may be imposed by local, state, or federal authorities. For example, unauthorized water extraction can incur fines that range from hundreds to thousands of dollars, depending on the severity of the violation.

- **Legal Action:** Non-compliance can also lead to legal action from affected parties, such as neighboring landowners or environmental organizations. This can result in costly litigation and potential damages.

- **Environmental Degradation:** Unsustainable water extraction practices can lead to environmental degradation, such as the depletion of aquifers, reduced water quality, and negative impacts on local flora and fauna. This not only affects the ecosystem but can also lead to stricter regulations in the future.

Examples of Compliance Strategies

To ensure compliance with local health and environmental regulations, consider implementing the following strategies:

- **Conduct Thorough Research:** Before beginning any water harvesting project, conduct thorough research to understand the specific regulations that apply to your area. This may include reviewing local government websites, consulting with local water authorities, and seeking advice from legal experts specializing in water rights.

- **Obtain Necessary Permits:** If your project requires permits, ensure that you apply for and obtain them before commencing any work. This may involve submitting detailed plans of your water harvesting system and demonstrating how it will comply with local regulations.

- **Engage with Local Authorities:** Establish a relationship with local water management authorities. This can provide valuable insights into best practices for water harvesting and help you stay informed about any changes in regulations.

- **Implement Best Practices:** Adopt best practices for sustainable water harvesting and management. This includes using appropriate filtration and purification methods to ensure water quality, as well as maintaining records of your water usage and any maintenance performed on your systems.

Conclusion

Complying with local health and environmental regulations is a fundamental aspect of responsible water harvesting. By understanding the legal framework, recognizing the potential problems associated with non-compliance, and implementing effective compliance strategies, you can ensure that your underground water harvesting practices are sustainable, legal, and beneficial to both you and the environment. Remember, proactive engagement with local authorities and adherence to regulations not only protects your interests but also

PERMITTING AND LEGAL CONSIDERATIONS

contributes to the broader goal of sustainable water management in your community.

Consulting Legal Experts for Water-related Issues

In navigating the complex landscape of water rights and regulations, consulting legal experts is crucial for ensuring compliance and protecting your interests. Water-related issues can encompass a range of legal concerns, including water rights, access to water sources, extraction permits, and environmental regulations. This section will explore the importance of legal consultation, common legal challenges, and how to effectively engage with legal professionals.

The Importance of Legal Consultation

Water is a vital resource, and its management is often subject to intricate laws and regulations that vary by jurisdiction. Legal experts specializing in water law can provide invaluable guidance on the following aspects:

- **Understanding Water Rights:** Water rights determine who can use water from a particular source and under what conditions. Legal experts can help clarify whether you have riparian rights (rights associated with land adjacent to water bodies) or prior appropriation rights (rights based on first usage).

- **Navigating Permitting Processes:** Many jurisdictions require permits for water extraction, especially for large-scale operations. A legal expert can help you understand the application process, necessary documentation, and potential challenges.

- **Compliance with Environmental Regulations:** Water extraction and usage must often comply with environmental laws aimed at protecting ecosystems. Legal guidance can ensure that your practices do not violate regulations that protect endangered species, wetlands, or water quality standards.

Common Legal Challenges

Engaging with water-related legal matters can present various challenges. Some common issues include:

- **Disputes Over Water Rights:** Conflicts can arise between neighboring landowners over water usage. Legal experts can assist in mediating disputes and representing your interests in court if necessary.

- **Regulatory Changes:** Water laws are subject to change based on new policies or environmental considerations. Staying informed about these changes through legal counsel can help you adapt your practices accordingly.
- **Environmental Compliance:** Failing to comply with environmental regulations can lead to significant penalties. Legal experts can help you develop compliance strategies and represent you in the event of enforcement actions.

Engaging with Legal Professionals

To effectively consult with legal experts on water-related issues, consider the following steps:

1. **Identify the Right Specialist:** Look for attorneys who specialize in water law, environmental law, or property rights. Their expertise will ensure that you receive informed guidance tailored to your specific situation.

2. **Prepare Relevant Documentation:** Gather all pertinent documents, such as property deeds, previous water usage records, and any correspondence with regulatory agencies. This information will help your legal counsel assess your situation effectively.

3. **Ask Questions:** During your consultation, ask specific questions about your rights, potential risks, and the implications of various legal options. Understanding your position will empower you to make informed decisions.

4. **Follow Up:** Legal matters can evolve over time. Maintain communication with your legal expert to stay updated on any changes that may affect your water rights or extraction processes.

Case Study Example

Consider a hypothetical case where a landowner discovers an underground spring on their property. The landowner wishes to utilize this water source for irrigation but is uncertain about the legal implications. Consulting a water law attorney, the landowner learns about the following:

- **Water Rights Assessment:** The attorney explains that the landowner may have riparian rights, allowing them to access the spring, but they must also consider local regulations governing water extraction.

- **Permit Requirements:** The attorney advises that a permit is necessary for large-scale water extraction to ensure compliance with state regulations. They assist in preparing the application and gathering required documentation.

- **Environmental Considerations:** The attorney highlights potential environmental impacts of irrigation and recommends conducting an environmental assessment to avoid future legal complications.

Through this consultation, the landowner gains clarity on their rights and responsibilities, enabling them to proceed with confidence while minimizing legal risks.

Conclusion

Consulting legal experts for water-related issues is not merely advisable; it is essential for anyone looking to responsibly manage water resources. By understanding water rights, navigating permitting processes, and ensuring compliance with environmental regulations, individuals can protect their interests and contribute to sustainable water management practices. Engaging with knowledgeable legal professionals will provide the necessary support to navigate the complexities of water law and ensure that your water usage is both legal and ethical.

Emergency Situations and Contingency Plans

Dealing with Water Scarcity and Drought

Water Conservation Strategies

Water conservation is critical in survival situations, especially during periods of water scarcity and drought. Implementing effective water conservation strategies can significantly extend the availability of water resources. This section outlines various methods and practices to conserve water efficiently.

Understanding Water Usage

To effectively conserve water, it is essential first to understand how it is used. The average person consumes approximately 80 to 100 gallons of water per day for various activities, including drinking, cooking, bathing, and irrigation. By assessing individual and household water usage, one can identify areas where conservation efforts can be most effective.

$$\text{Total Daily Water Usage} = \sum_{i=1}^{n} \text{Usage}_i \tag{75}$$

where Usage_i represents the water used for each activity i (e.g., drinking, bathing, cleaning, etc.), and n is the total number of activities.

Implementing Efficient Practices

1. **Reduce, Reuse, and Recycle**: The three R's are fundamental principles in water conservation. Reducing water use involves minimizing waste, while reusing water (such as using greywater from sinks for irrigation) can significantly lower

overall consumption. Recycling water involves treating and reusing wastewater for non-potable applications.

2. **Install Water-Efficient Fixtures**: Upgrading to low-flow faucets, showerheads, and toilets can drastically reduce water usage without sacrificing performance. For example, a low-flow showerhead can save up to 2.5 gallons per minute compared to traditional models.

3. **Use Water-Saving Appliances**: Dishwashers and washing machines that are rated for water efficiency can save significant amounts of water. These appliances often use less water than handwashing dishes or doing laundry in older machines.

Behavioral Changes

1. **Mindful Water Use**: Encourage individuals to be mindful of their water consumption. Simple actions such as turning off the tap while brushing teeth, taking shorter showers, and using a broom instead of a hose to clean driveways can contribute to significant water savings.

2. **Irrigation Practices**: In agricultural settings, implementing drip irrigation systems can reduce water usage by delivering water directly to the plant roots, minimizing evaporation and runoff. Timing irrigation for early morning or late evening can also reduce water loss due to evaporation.

3. **Mulching and Xeriscaping**: In landscaping, using mulch around plants can retain soil moisture and reduce the need for frequent watering. Xeriscaping involves designing landscapes to be drought-resistant, utilizing native plants that require less water.

Monitoring and Maintenance

Regularly monitoring water usage can help identify leaks and inefficiencies. For example, a leaking faucet can waste approximately 3,000 gallons of water per year.

$$\text{Annual Water Waste} = \text{Leak Rate} \times \text{Time} \tag{76}$$

where Leak Rate is the volume of water lost per minute, and Time is the total time the leak persists in minutes.

Community Involvement

Engaging the community in water conservation efforts can amplify the impact. Organizing workshops on water-saving techniques, establishing community gardens with efficient irrigation systems, and promoting local policies that support water conservation can foster a culture of sustainability.

Education and Awareness

Educating individuals about the importance of water conservation and the impact of their actions on local water resources is crucial. Awareness campaigns can highlight the benefits of conservation and provide actionable tips for reducing water usage.

Conclusion

Implementing water conservation strategies is vital for ensuring water availability during scarcity. By understanding water usage, adopting efficient practices, encouraging behavioral changes, monitoring consumption, and fostering community involvement, individuals can significantly contribute to water conservation efforts. These strategies not only help in survival situations but also promote sustainable living practices that benefit the environment and future generations.

Finding Alternative Water Sources in Arid Environments

In arid environments, the scarcity of surface water sources necessitates innovative strategies for finding alternative water supplies. This section will explore various methods to identify and harvest water in regions characterized by low precipitation and high evaporation rates.

Understanding the Challenges

Arid climates pose significant challenges to water availability. The average annual rainfall in arid regions can be less than 250 mm, leading to prolonged periods of drought and a reliance on limited water sources. The high evaporation rates, often exceeding 2000 mm annually, further exacerbate water scarcity. Consequently, residents and survivalists must employ alternative strategies to secure water.

Identifying Potential Water Sources

1. **Groundwater Exploration** Groundwater is often a vital resource in arid regions. To locate groundwater, consider the following techniques:

    - **Hydrogeological Mapping:** Use geological maps to identify aquifer locations. Look for formations such as sandstone, limestone, and gravel, which typically store and transmit water effectively.

- **Dowsing:** While not scientifically proven, some individuals claim success in locating groundwater through dowsing techniques involving divining rods.

- **Geophysical Surveys:** Employ resistivity and seismic surveys to detect underground water. These methods measure the electrical resistance of soil and rock, allowing for the identification of water-saturated zones.

2. Rainwater Harvesting In arid environments, capturing and storing rainwater during infrequent precipitation events can provide a critical water supply. Consider the following methods:

- **Surface Catchment Systems:** Construct catchment areas using impermeable materials to direct rainwater into storage tanks. A simple equation to estimate the volume of water collected is:

$$V = A \times P \qquad (77)$$

where V is the volume of water (in liters), A is the area of the catchment surface (in square meters), and P is the precipitation (in meters).

- **Gutters and Downspouts:** Install gutters on buildings to channel rainwater into storage barrels or cisterns. Ensure that the system is equipped with filters to remove debris and contaminants.

- **Permeable Pavements:** Utilize permeable surfaces for driveways and walkways to allow rainwater infiltration into the ground, enhancing groundwater recharge.

3. Utilizing Vegetation Certain plants can serve as indicators of underground water sources. The presence of specific vegetation types often suggests proximity to water. For instance:

- **Willows and Cottonwoods:** These trees thrive near water sources and can indicate groundwater presence.

- **Cacti and Succulents:** These plants store water in their tissues and can provide moisture when consumed. However, caution is advised, as not all species are safe for human consumption.

Innovative Water Extraction Techniques

In arid environments, traditional methods may not suffice. Therefore, consider innovative techniques for extracting water:

1. Atmospheric Water Generation Atmospheric water generators (AWGs) utilize humidity in the air to produce potable water. These devices condense moisture from the atmosphere, making them particularly useful in arid regions with high humidity levels, such as coastal deserts.

2. Fog Nets In some arid regions, fog nets can be employed to capture moisture from fog. These nets are designed to condense water droplets from fog, which then drip into collection containers. This method has proven effective in places like the Atacama Desert in Chile, where fog is prevalent.

3. Desalination In coastal arid regions, desalination can provide a viable alternative water source. While energy-intensive, advancements in technology have made desalination more efficient and cost-effective. Reverse osmosis and solar desalination are two common methods employed to convert seawater into potable water.

Conclusion

Finding alternative water sources in arid environments is critical for survival and sustainability. By leveraging groundwater exploration, rainwater harvesting, vegetation indicators, and innovative extraction techniques, individuals can secure essential water supplies. Understanding the unique challenges posed by arid climates and employing a multifaceted approach will enhance water availability and resilience in these regions. Continuous research and adaptation of methods will further improve water management strategies in the face of climate change and increasing water scarcity.

Developing Contingency Plans for Water Shortages

In the face of increasing climate variability and the potential for water scarcity, developing a contingency plan for water shortages is essential for survival and sustainability. This section outlines the theoretical framework, identifies potential problems, and provides actionable strategies for creating effective contingency plans.

Understanding Water Scarcity

Water scarcity occurs when the demand for water exceeds the available supply. This can be due to natural factors such as drought, or human-induced factors such as over-extraction of groundwater or pollution. The United Nations defines water scarcity as occurring when water availability falls below 1,700 cubic meters per person per year. Understanding the dynamics of water scarcity is crucial for developing effective contingency plans.

Key Components of a Contingency Plan

A well-structured contingency plan for water shortages should include the following key components:

- **Assessment of Current Water Resources:** Evaluate available water sources, including surface water, groundwater, and rainwater harvesting systems. Conduct a water audit to determine current usage and identify areas for conservation.

- **Identification of Water Needs:** Calculate the minimum water requirements for essential activities such as drinking, cooking, sanitation, and hygiene. The World Health Organization (WHO) recommends a minimum of 15 liters per person per day for basic needs.

- **Contingency Strategies:** Develop strategies for reducing water use during shortages, including prioritizing essential needs, implementing water rationing, and utilizing alternative water sources.

- **Monitoring and Evaluation:** Establish a system for monitoring water supply and demand, and evaluate the effectiveness of implemented strategies regularly.

Calculating Water Needs

To effectively manage water resources during shortages, it is essential to quantify water needs. The following equation can be used to estimate daily water requirements:

$$W = P \times R \tag{78}$$

Where:

- W = Total water requirement (liters per day)
- P = Number of people in the household or community
- R = Recommended water use per person (liters per day)

For example, for a household of four people:

$$W = 4 \times 15 = 60 \text{ liters per day} \tag{79}$$

Strategies for Water Conservation

Implementing water conservation strategies is critical in mitigating the impact of shortages. Some effective strategies include:

- **Fixing Leaks:** Regularly inspect and repair leaks in pipes and fixtures to prevent water loss.
- **Using Water-Efficient Fixtures:** Install low-flow faucets, showerheads, and dual-flush toilets to reduce water consumption.
- **Rainwater Harvesting:** Collect and store rainwater for non-potable uses, such as irrigation and toilet flushing.
- **Recycling Greywater:** Implement systems to reuse greywater from sinks, showers, and laundry for irrigation or toilet flushing.

Contingency Measures for Drought Conditions

In areas prone to drought, additional contingency measures should be considered:

- **Water Rationing:** Establish a water rationing plan that specifies the amount of water allocated per person per day based on the severity of the shortage.
- **Community Engagement:** Involve the community in water conservation efforts through education and awareness campaigns.
- **Alternative Water Sources:** Identify alternative sources of water, such as desalination, if applicable, or transport water from other regions if feasible.

Emergency Water Supplies

Stockpiling emergency water supplies can provide a buffer during acute shortages. Guidelines for emergency water storage include:

- **Container Selection:** Use food-grade water storage containers to prevent contamination.

- **Storage Location:** Store water in a cool, dark place to inhibit algae growth and contamination.

- **Rotation Schedule:** Implement a rotation schedule to ensure stored water is used and replaced regularly, ideally every six months.

Scenario Planning

Developing different scenarios for potential water shortages can enhance preparedness. Consider the following scenarios:

- **Short-term Drought:** Plan for a 30-day drought with a gradual reduction in water supply.

- **Long-term Water Scarcity:** Assess the implications of a prolonged drought lasting several months or years, requiring significant lifestyle changes.

- **Natural Disasters:** Prepare for sudden disruptions caused by floods or contamination events, necessitating immediate access to emergency supplies.

Conclusion

Developing a comprehensive contingency plan for water shortages is essential for ensuring access to this vital resource in times of crisis. By assessing current resources, calculating water needs, implementing conservation strategies, and preparing for emergencies, individuals and communities can enhance their resilience against water scarcity. With proactive planning and community engagement, the impacts of water shortages can be effectively mitigated, safeguarding health and well-being.

Implementing Emergency Water Rationing Measures

In situations of water scarcity, effective water rationing becomes a critical strategy to ensure that available water resources are utilized efficiently and equitably. Rationing involves the controlled distribution of water to meet the needs of a population while conserving supplies for the long term. This section outlines the theory behind water rationing, identifies potential problems, and provides actionable examples to guide implementation.

Understanding Water Rationing

Water rationing is a systematic approach to managing limited water supplies during emergencies such as droughts, natural disasters, or infrastructure failures. The primary goal is to extend the available water supply while prioritizing essential needs. The theoretical foundation of water rationing can be expressed through the following equation:

$$W_r = \frac{W_a}{N} \qquad (80)$$

Where:

- W_r = Rationed water per person (liters per day)
- W_a = Available water supply (liters)
- N = Total number of individuals in need

This equation highlights the direct relationship between the available water supply and the number of individuals relying on it. As the number of individuals increases or the available water supply decreases, the rationed amount per person also decreases.

Challenges in Water Rationing

Several challenges may arise during the implementation of water rationing measures:

- **Equity and Fairness:** Ensuring that all individuals receive a fair share of water is paramount. Disparities in distribution can lead to conflicts and dissatisfaction among the population.
- **Monitoring Usage:** Accurately tracking water usage is essential to prevent overuse and ensure compliance with rationing measures. This requires effective monitoring systems and community engagement.

- **Behavioral Change:** Changing water usage habits can be difficult. Individuals may resist rationing measures, leading to non-compliance and increased stress on water resources.

- **Emergency Response:** Rapidly changing conditions, such as natural disasters, can complicate rationing efforts. Flexibility in the system is crucial to adapt to evolving situations.

Steps for Implementing Water Rationing

To implement effective water rationing measures, follow these actionable steps:

1. Assess Available Water Supply Begin by evaluating the total available water supply. This includes surface water, groundwater, and any stored water reserves. Accurate assessment is crucial for determining the amount of water that can be rationed.

2. Determine Essential Needs Identify the essential needs of the population, including drinking, cooking, sanitation, and hygiene. A common guideline is to allocate a minimum of 2 to 4 liters per person per day for drinking and cooking, while additional water may be needed for hygiene purposes.

3. Calculate Rationing Levels Using Equation (1), calculate the rationed amount of water per person. Adjust the figures based on the specific needs of vulnerable populations, such as children, the elderly, and individuals with medical conditions.

4. Communicate Rationing Measures Clearly communicate the rationing measures to the community. Use various platforms, such as community meetings, flyers, and social media, to ensure that everyone understands the importance of rationing and how it will be implemented.

5. Establish Monitoring Systems Implement monitoring systems to track water usage and compliance. This may involve regular reporting from households or the installation of flow meters in community water distribution points.

6. Encourage Conservation Practices Promote water conservation practices within the community. This can include educational campaigns on water-saving techniques, such as fixing leaks, using water-efficient appliances, and practicing mindful consumption.

7. Review and Adapt Rationing Strategies Regularly review the effectiveness of the rationing measures and adapt them as necessary. This may involve adjusting rationing levels based on changes in water availability or community needs.

Case Studies of Successful Water Rationing

Examining successful case studies can provide valuable insights into effective water rationing strategies:

Case Study 1: Cape Town, South Africa During the severe drought of 2017-2018, Cape Town implemented a water rationing program that effectively reduced consumption. The city set a target of 500 liters per person per day and encouraged residents to adopt water-saving measures. By promoting awareness and community engagement, Cape Town successfully reduced water usage by 50%.

Case Study 2: São Paulo, Brazil In response to water shortages, São Paulo introduced a tiered pricing system for water consumption. Households that exceeded their allotted water usage faced higher rates, incentivizing conservation. This approach not only reduced consumption but also raised funds for water infrastructure improvements.

Conclusion

Implementing emergency water rationing measures is a vital response to water scarcity. By understanding the theoretical framework, addressing challenges, and following actionable steps, communities can effectively manage limited water resources. Learning from successful case studies further enhances the ability to adapt and thrive in the face of water-related emergencies.

Through proactive planning and community involvement, water rationing can safeguard essential water supplies, ensuring that all individuals have access to the resources they need for survival.

Natural Disasters and Other Emergencies

Preparing for Floods and Water Contamination

Floods are one of the most common and devastating natural disasters, capable of causing significant damage to infrastructure, homes, and, importantly, water sources. Understanding how to prepare for floods and mitigate the risk of water contamination is crucial for survival in such emergencies.

Understanding Flood Dynamics

Flooding occurs when water overflows onto normally dry land. This can be caused by heavy rainfall, melting snow, or a combination of both. The dynamics of flooding can be understood through the following key concepts:

- **Hydrological Cycle:** The continuous movement of water on, above, and below the surface of the Earth. Floods can disrupt this cycle, leading to contamination of water sources.

- **Flood Zones:** Areas that are prone to flooding, often identified through historical data. Understanding these zones can help in preparing for potential flooding events.

- **Runoff and Infiltration:** During heavy rainfall, the rate of runoff increases, while infiltration decreases. This can lead to surface water accumulation and potential flooding.

Identifying Risks of Water Contamination

Floodwaters can carry a range of contaminants, making it unsafe for consumption. Common contaminants include:

- **Pathogens:** Bacteria, viruses, and parasites can enter water sources through sewage overflow or animal waste.

- **Chemicals:** Agricultural runoff, industrial waste, and household chemicals can pollute water during floods.

- **Sediments:** Soil and debris washed into water sources can harbor contaminants and affect water quality.

Preparation Strategies

To prepare for floods and minimize the risk of water contamination, consider the following strategies:

1. **Risk Assessment**   Conduct a thorough assessment of your property and community to identify flood risks. This includes:

    + Mapping flood zones and understanding local flood history.

    + Identifying vulnerable areas such as basements and low-lying regions.

    + Evaluating the proximity of your water sources to potential contaminants.

2. **Water Storage Solutions**   Implement water storage solutions that can withstand flooding:

    + **Elevate Water Storage Tanks:** Ensure that any water storage tanks are elevated above potential flood levels.

    + **Use Sealed Containers:** Store water in sealed, food-grade containers to prevent contamination from floodwaters.

    + **Backup Water Supplies:** Consider having a backup supply of bottled water that is stored in a safe, elevated location.

3. **Emergency Preparedness Plans**   Develop an emergency preparedness plan that includes:

    + **Evacuation Routes:** Identify safe evacuation routes away from flood-prone areas.

    + **Communication Plans:** Establish a communication plan with family and friends to stay informed during a flood event.

    + **Emergency Kits:** Assemble emergency kits that include water purification tablets, filters, and other water treatment supplies.

Mitigation Techniques

In addition to preparation, employing mitigation techniques can help reduce the impact of floods:

1. Landscaping Solutions Utilize landscaping techniques to manage water flow:

- **Rain Gardens:** Create rain gardens that can absorb excess water and reduce runoff.

- **Swales:** Implement swales (shallow ditches) to direct water away from structures and towards absorption areas.

2. Flood Barriers Install flood barriers around your property to prevent water intrusion:

- **Sandbags:** Use sandbags to create temporary barriers during flood warnings.

- **Permanent Barriers:** Consider investing in permanent flood barriers for long-term protection.

Post-Flood Water Safety

After a flood event, it is essential to assess water safety before consumption:

1. Water Testing Conduct water quality testing to identify contaminants. Testing can include:

- **Microbial Testing:** Check for the presence of pathogens.

- **Chemical Testing:** Analyze for harmful chemicals and heavy metals.

2. Water Purification Methods Use appropriate purification methods if contamination is detected:

- **Boiling:** Boil water for at least one minute to kill pathogens.

- **Filtration:** Use water filters designed to remove bacteria and protozoa.

- **Chemical Treatment:** Apply water purification tablets or bleach (2 drops per liter) to disinfect water.

Conclusion

Preparing for floods and potential water contamination is essential for ensuring access to safe drinking water during emergencies. By understanding flood dynamics, assessing risks, implementing preparation strategies, and employing mitigation techniques, individuals and communities can significantly enhance their resilience against flooding and its associated challenges. Regularly reviewing and updating emergency plans will further ensure readiness for any unforeseen circumstances.

$$\text{Water Safety} = \text{Preparation} + \text{Testing} + \text{Purification} \qquad (81)$$

Managing Water Supplies during Power Outages

Power outages can significantly disrupt water supply systems, especially in areas where water is pumped from underground sources or treated at municipal facilities. Understanding how to manage water supplies during these outages is crucial for maintaining access to safe drinking water and ensuring proper hygiene.

Understanding the Impact of Power Outages on Water Supply

During a power outage, water supply systems may face several challenges:

- **Pump Failures:** Most modern water systems rely on electric pumps to draw water from wells or reservoirs. Without electricity, these pumps cannot operate, leading to immediate water shortages.

- **Water Treatment Disruption:** Water treatment facilities often depend on electricity to operate filtration and disinfection systems. A power outage can halt these processes, risking water contamination.

- **Increased Demand:** In emergencies, the demand for water may increase as people stockpile supplies, further straining available resources.

Assessing Water Storage Capacity

To manage water supplies effectively during power outages, it is essential to assess your available water storage capacity. This includes both the amount of water stored in tanks or cisterns and the capacity of any backup systems.

$$\text{Total Water Storage} = \sum_{i=1}^{n} V_i \qquad (82)$$

Where V_i is the volume of each storage container and n is the total number of containers. Ensure that your storage capacity meets your household's needs, which can be estimated using the following guideline:

$$\text{Daily Water Needs} = \text{Number of People} \times 3.785 \text{ L/person} \qquad (83)$$

This formula assumes a daily requirement of approximately 3.785 liters (1 gallon) of water per person for drinking and basic hygiene.

Implementing Water Conservation Strategies

During a power outage, conserving water becomes paramount. Here are several strategies to reduce water usage:

- **Limit Flushing:** Avoid flushing toilets unnecessarily. Consider using a bucket for flushing if needed.

- **Shorten Showers:** Reduce shower times and consider sponge baths to conserve water.

- **Reuse Water:** Collect and reuse water from cooking or washing vegetables for flushing toilets or watering plants.

Alternative Water Sources

In addition to stored water, identifying alternative water sources can be crucial during power outages. Consider the following options:

- **Rainwater Harvesting:** If you have a rainwater collection system, ensure it is clean and ready for use. Rainwater can be an excellent source for non-potable uses, such as flushing toilets and irrigation.

- **Natural Water Sources:** If safe and accessible, nearby rivers, lakes, or streams can be used. Always purify this water before consumption using methods such as boiling or filtration.

Emergency Water Rationing

In extreme cases where water supply is limited, implementing a rationing system may be necessary. This can help ensure that available water lasts longer during outages.

$$\text{Rationed Water Supply} = \frac{\text{Total Water Storage}}{\text{Days Until Power Restoration}} \quad (84)$$

This equation provides a daily limit on water usage per person, allowing for equitable distribution among household members.

Preparing for Future Outages

To better prepare for future power outages, consider the following proactive measures:

- **Install Backup Systems:** Consider investing in a generator to power essential water systems during outages. Solar-powered pumps can also provide a sustainable alternative.

- **Regular Maintenance:** Ensure that all water storage systems, pumps, and treatment facilities are regularly maintained to minimize the risk of failure during emergencies.

- **Educate Household Members:** Teach all household members about water conservation techniques and emergency procedures to ensure everyone knows how to manage water supplies effectively during outages.

By understanding the challenges posed by power outages and implementing effective management strategies, individuals and communities can maintain access to safe water supplies, ensuring health and hygiene even in difficult circumstances.

Assessing and Responding to Water-Related Disasters

Water-related disasters can manifest in various forms, including floods, hurricanes, tsunamis, and severe storms. These events can lead to significant threats to public health, safety, and infrastructure. Understanding how to assess and respond to these disasters is crucial for effective management and recovery.

Understanding the Nature of Water-Related Disasters

Water-related disasters are characterized by the excessive presence of water in areas where it can cause harm. For instance, flooding occurs when water overflows from rivers, lakes, or drainage systems, inundating surrounding land. The Federal Emergency Management Agency (FEMA) defines a flood as a temporary condition where two or more acres of normally dry land are inundated by water.

The impact of such disasters can be quantified using the following equation that estimates the potential damage caused by flooding:

$$D = P \times A \times C \qquad (85)$$

where:

- D = Total damage cost
- P = Average cost per unit area (e.g., cost of property and infrastructure)
- A = Area affected by the disaster (in square miles or acres)
- C = Damage coefficient (a factor representing the severity of the disaster, ranging from 0 to 1)

For example, if a flood affects an area of 10 acres, with an average cost of $10,000 per acre, and a damage coefficient of 0.5, the total damage would be calculated as follows:

$$D = 10,000 \times 10 \times 0.5 = 50,000$$

This simple model illustrates the economic implications of water-related disasters, emphasizing the need for preparedness and response strategies.

Assessing Risks and Vulnerabilities

The first step in responding to water-related disasters is to assess the risks and vulnerabilities of the area. This involves:

- **Identifying High-Risk Areas:** Use historical data to identify regions prone to flooding or other water-related disasters. Geographic Information Systems (GIS) can be instrumental in visualizing these areas.

- **Evaluating Infrastructure Resilience:** Assess the condition of existing infrastructure, such as levees, dams, and drainage systems. The failure of these structures can exacerbate the impacts of water-related disasters.

- **Analyzing Population Vulnerability:** Identify populations at risk, including low-income communities, the elderly, and individuals with disabilities. Understanding demographics can help tailor response efforts.

Implementing Response Strategies

Once risks are assessed, the next step is to implement effective response strategies:

- **Emergency Communication:** Establish a robust communication plan to disseminate information about the disaster. Utilize multiple channels such as social media, radio, and local news outlets to reach a broad audience.

- **Evacuation Plans:** Develop clear evacuation routes and procedures. Conduct drills to ensure that residents are familiar with these plans. It is crucial to have designated shelters that can accommodate evacuees.

- **Resource Allocation:** Mobilize resources such as food, water, medical supplies, and personnel. Establish partnerships with local organizations and agencies to facilitate resource distribution.

- **Public Health Initiatives:** Implement measures to prevent waterborne diseases following a disaster. This includes providing access to clean drinking water, sanitation facilities, and health services.

Post-Disaster Recovery and Assessment

After the immediate response phase, focus shifts to recovery and long-term assessment:

- **Damage Assessment:** Conduct a thorough assessment of the damage to infrastructure and property. This information is vital for securing federal and state disaster relief funds.

- **Restoration of Services:** Prioritize the restoration of essential services such as water supply, electricity, and transportation. Collaborate with utility companies and local governments to expedite recovery efforts.

- **Community Engagement:** Involve the community in recovery efforts. This can foster resilience and ensure that recovery plans meet the needs of affected residents.

- **Mitigation Strategies:** Post-disaster is an opportune time to evaluate and enhance mitigation strategies. This includes revisiting land-use planning, strengthening infrastructure, and implementing natural solutions like wetland restoration.

Case Studies

To illustrate these principles in action, consider the following case studies:

Case Study 1: Hurricane Katrina (2005) Hurricane Katrina showcased the catastrophic impacts of water-related disasters. New Orleans experienced severe flooding due to levee failures. The response was hampered by inadequate communication and evacuation plans, leading to significant loss of life and property. Post-disaster, the city implemented stricter building codes and improved emergency response protocols, focusing on community engagement and resilience.

Case Study 2: The 2010 Pakistan Floods The 2010 floods in Pakistan affected millions, leading to widespread displacement and health crises. The government, with support from international organizations, implemented emergency response measures, including the distribution of clean water and medical supplies. Recovery efforts focused on rebuilding infrastructure and enhancing flood management systems to mitigate future risks.

Conclusion

Assessing and responding to water-related disasters requires a comprehensive approach that encompasses risk assessment, emergency response, and long-term recovery strategies. By understanding the nature of these disasters and implementing effective measures, communities can enhance their resilience and minimize the impacts of future events. Continuous learning from past disasters and integrating innovative solutions will be key to building a sustainable future in the face of climate change and increasing water-related threats.

Stockpiling Emergency Water Supplies

In any survival situation, access to clean water is critical. Therefore, stockpiling emergency water supplies is an essential strategy for ensuring that you and your family can withstand periods of water scarcity, whether due to natural disasters, infrastructure failures, or other emergencies. This section outlines the key considerations and strategies for effectively stockpiling water supplies.

NATURAL DISASTERS AND OTHER EMERGENCIES

Understanding Water Needs

The average person requires approximately 2 to 3 liters of water per day for drinking, cooking, and hygiene. In emergency situations, the demand may increase due to stress, heat, and physical exertion. Therefore, it is recommended to stockpile at least one gallon (approximately 3.78 liters) of water per person per day. This estimate allows for both consumption and hygiene needs.

$$\text{Total Water Supply (in gallons)} = \text{Number of People} \times \text{Days of Supply} \times 1 \text{ gallon} \tag{86}$$

For example, a family of four preparing for a two-week emergency would need:

$$\text{Total Water Supply} = 4 \text{ people} \times 14 \text{ days} \times 1 \text{ gallon} = 56 \text{ gallons} \tag{87}$$

Choosing the Right Containers

When stockpiling water, it is vital to use appropriate containers to ensure the water remains safe for consumption. Containers should be:

- **Food-grade:** Use containers specifically designed for water storage, such as those labeled as food-safe.

- **Durable:** Choose containers that can withstand pressure and temperature fluctuations without degrading.

- **Sealable:** Ensure containers have tight-fitting lids to prevent contamination and evaporation.

Common options include:

- **Water barrels:** Typically hold 55 gallons and are suitable for long-term storage.

- **5-gallon jugs:** Easier to handle and transport, ideal for smaller stockpiles.

- **Plastic bottles:** Useful for short-term storage and easy to distribute.

Water Treatment and Purification

Before storing water, it is essential to treat it to prevent contamination. If using tap water, it is usually treated and safe for storage. However, if using well water or surface water, it must be purified. Here are some methods:

- **Boiling**: Bring water to a rolling boil for at least one minute to kill pathogens.
- **Chemical treatment**: Use water purification tablets or household bleach (5-9
- **Filtration**: Use a water filter designed to remove bacteria and protozoa.

Storage Conditions

Store water in a cool, dark place to minimize the growth of algae and bacteria. Ideal storage temperatures range from 50°F to 70°F (10°C to 21°C). Avoid direct sunlight, which can degrade plastic containers and promote algae growth.

Rotation and Maintenance

Regularly check and rotate your water supplies to ensure freshness. It is recommended to replace stored water every six months to a year. Mark containers with the date of storage for easy tracking.

Emergency Access and Distribution

In an emergency, ensure that water supplies are easily accessible. Store water in multiple locations within your home to facilitate quick access during an emergency. Consider creating a distribution plan for your family, assigning specific roles to ensure that everyone knows where the water is stored and how to access it.

Example of a Stockpile Plan

To illustrate a stockpiling plan, consider the following example for a family of four preparing for a two-week emergency:

- **Daily Requirement**: 1 gallon per person
- **Total Requirement**: 56 gallons
- **Storage Containers**:
    - 2 x 30-gallon barrels (60 gallons total)

- **Water Treatment:**

    - Treat with bleach before filling barrels.

- **Storage Location:**

    - Basement or cool closet, away from sunlight.

In conclusion, stockpiling emergency water supplies is a proactive measure that can significantly enhance your preparedness for unexpected situations. By calculating your water needs, selecting appropriate containers, treating and maintaining your water supply, and ensuring easy access, you can secure a vital resource that sustains life during emergencies.

Index

-bearing rock, 15
-effectiveness, 12

a, 2–5, 9–12, 15–22, 24, 27, 29–39, 42, 44–46, 48–57, 59–61, 63–72, 74, 75, 77–83, 85, 88–92, 94, 95, 97, 98, 100–107, 109–112, 115, 116, 119, 123, 125–128, 130, 131, 133, 136–138, 140, 142, 143, 145–148, 150–154, 158–161, 163–173, 176–179
ability, 11–13, 15, 20, 27, 66, 89, 102, 167
absorption, 50
access, 3–5, 7, 10–12, 17, 19, 21, 22, 36, 42, 49, 67, 68, 97, 99, 107, 117, 120, 122, 128, 136, 140, 145–147, 151, 153, 164, 167, 171, 173, 176, 178, 179
accessibility, 12, 18, 22, 23, 25–27, 48, 50, 63, 105
account, 64
accuracy, 138
acidity, 136
action, 88, 89, 176

activity, 1, 21, 31, 136
adaptation, 161
addition, 127, 169, 172
address, 71, 97, 111, 125
adherence, 115, 152
affordability, 105
age, 1
aid, 15
air, 9, 94, 95, 101
algae, 68, 123–126
alkalinity, 136
alternative, 11, 65, 159, 161, 172
amber, 3
amount, 1, 20, 50, 75, 78, 103, 165, 166, 171
analysis, 19, 30, 136
analyze, 18
anode, 118
application, 89, 102, 109, 110, 112, 114, 149, 150
approach, 38, 51, 71, 72, 74, 80, 91, 97, 111, 130, 161, 165, 167, 176
appropriation, 147
aquifer, 14, 15, 17, 19, 50, 129
area, 13–15, 18, 19, 21, 29–31, 42, 45, 49, 54, 55, 57, 64, 65, 68, 75, 78, 80, 85, 103,

181

104, 110, 112, 148, 174
array, 104
arsenal, 117
aspect, 65, 152
assessment, 27, 137, 166, 169, 175, 176
assistance, 70
atmosphere, 40, 95, 96
attach, 118
attorney, 154
autonomy, 79
availability, 12–15, 18, 20, 22, 49, 72, 74, 83, 94, 96, 120, 136, 157, 159, 161, 162, 167
awareness, 39

bacteria, 21, 38, 110, 112, 118, 127, 133, 137
bailer, 101
balance, 17
barrier, 49
base, 30, 67
basement, 74, 128
basin, 54
bathing, 157
bed, 31, 110
behavior, 42
being, 3, 5, 44, 48, 51, 67, 71, 115, 138, 164
belief, 101
benefit, 11, 159
Bernoulli, 98
block, 67
body, 2, 3, 21
bottom, 81
box, 35
breakthrough, 111
brick, 66, 67

buffer, 12, 164
building, 51, 53, 54, 176

calendar, 127
California, 147
camping, 39
capacity, 67, 78–80, 84, 94, 129, 171
capture, 35, 46, 49–51, 56, 95, 96, 110, 147, 161
carbon, 83, 111
cartridge, 112
case, 34, 85, 154, 167, 176
catchment, 49, 54–57, 75, 78, 80
cause, 115, 133
cellulose, 110
center, 74
change, 14, 97, 105, 146, 161, 176
channel, 35, 49
check, 69, 127, 178
chemical, 25, 27, 39, 96, 111–115, 118, 123, 134, 136, 137, 141
chemistry, 118
Chile, 96, 161
chlorination, 83
chlorine, 118
choice, 45, 60, 63, 66, 110, 120
cholera, 141
cistern, 12, 63–69, 71, 74
city, 176
claim, 101
clarity, 39, 112, 134, 155
clay, 19, 42, 49
cleaning, 12, 69, 71, 124
cleanliness, 126
climate, 14, 20, 51, 56, 62, 96, 97, 131, 146, 161, 176
clogging, 111
coastal arid, 161

Index

coefficient, 78
coli, 21, 137
coliform, 137
collect, 12, 45, 46, 67, 78, 96, 101
collecting, 8, 44, 45, 47, 48, 75, 77, 95
collection, 9, 35, 45, 54, 56, 66, 74, 75, 77, 78, 80, 89, 91–96, 161
color, 3, 136
Colorado, 147
column, 98
combination, 31, 39, 83, 168
communication, 176
community, 17, 61, 74, 104, 111, 125, 126, 153, 158, 159, 164, 166, 167, 169, 176
compatibility, 85
competition, 22
compliance, 85, 147, 151–153, 155, 166
component, 4, 151
composition, 18, 42
concentration, 112, 137
concept, 83, 89
concern, 66, 138
conclusion, 3, 5, 15, 24, 31, 42, 48, 54, 56, 59, 94, 99, 179
concrete, 66, 67
condensation, 9, 40
condense, 161
conduct, 14, 30, 31, 69
conductivity, 49, 50
confidence, 155
connection, 143
conservation, 12, 44, 86, 105, 157–159, 163, 164, 166, 167
consideration, 51, 54, 65, 83, 91, 94

construct, 66
construction, 45, 51, 52, 54, 66–68
consultation, 15, 16, 153, 155
consulting, 15, 17, 65, 147, 153
consumption, 20, 21, 25, 31, 36, 37, 39, 78, 80, 81, 83, 112, 123, 126, 127, 136, 159, 166–168, 170, 177
contact, 112, 113
container, 35, 98, 105, 120, 126, 128
contaminant, 21, 90, 135
contamination, 11, 12, 20–22, 35, 69–71, 120, 123–127, 137, 168, 170, 171, 178
content, 92
context, 31, 54, 92
contingency, 161–164
continuity, 98
contour, 30
contrast, 10, 11, 30, 65
control, 51, 68
conversion, 97
convert, 161
cooking, 157, 166
cornerstone, 69
corrosion, 66
cost, 12, 83, 85, 116, 161
court, 146
cover, 15, 21, 80, 148
creation, 51
crisis, 164
cross, 19, 45
culture, 158
current, 13, 118, 164
custom, 66
cycle, 40
cylinder, 100

damage, 22, 68, 127, 167, 174

dampness, 30
Darcy, 45, 92
date, 127, 128, 178
day, 78, 79, 96, 104, 157, 166
death, 10
debris, 49, 67, 68, 111
decision, 138
degradation, 120
dehydration, 2, 3
demand, 22, 78, 80, 146, 162
density, 118
department, 17
depletion, 147
depth, 11, 13, 19, 45, 65, 67, 106, 110, 136
desalination, 9, 161
design, 17, 51, 52, 54, 56, 57, 59, 61, 75, 77, 80, 83, 100
designing, 51, 53, 54, 62, 77, 107
destination, 98
detail, 15, 97
detection, 125
development, 17, 39
device, 97
dew, 9, 95, 96
difference, 10, 98, 110
digging, 30, 105
diligence, 143
direction, 19
disaster, 176
discharge, 31, 32, 34
disease, 3–5
disinfectant, 112
disinfection, 39, 83, 112, 114–117, 134
displacement, 176
distribution, 18, 165, 166, 173, 176, 178
diverter, 85
do, 123, 147
doctrine, 147
dosage, 82
dowser, 101
dowsing, 101
drainage, 46, 54, 67
dredging, 12
drilling, 12
drinking, 21, 27, 38, 39, 97, 112, 117, 120, 126, 136, 140, 142, 157, 166, 171
drip, 95, 161
drop, 95, 111
drought, 11, 22, 49, 61, 71, 128, 130, 146, 157, 159, 162, 163
durability, 60, 66
duration, 116
dust, 127
dysentery, 141

Earth, 8, 39, 40
edge, 49
effect, 88
effectiveness, 12, 51, 53, 54, 57, 60, 74, 90, 96, 109, 110, 112, 113, 115, 116, 120, 167
efficacy, 113
efficiency, 54, 57, 61, 66, 72, 75, 77, 78, 80, 94, 96, 103, 105, 111, 118
effort, 21
electricity, 96, 99
electrocoagulation, 118
electroflotation, 118
electrooxidation, 118
element, 38, 110
elevation, 13, 30, 46, 97, 98, 101
emergency, 117, 128, 164, 167, 169, 171, 176–179

Index

employ, 159
end, 98, 101
energy, 9, 97, 101, 102, 105, 118, 161
engagement, 152, 164, 176
environment, 4, 7, 22, 25, 44, 69, 152, 159
equation, 11, 13, 21, 29, 31, 45, 55, 72, 75, 82, 88, 90, 94, 98, 103, 109, 110, 112, 115, 129, 162, 165, 173, 174
estimate, 56, 78, 162
evacuation, 176
evaluation, 34
evaporation, 10, 20, 40, 51, 57, 127, 159
event, 170
example, 12, 15, 21, 22, 49, 61, 78–81, 85, 89, 104, 146, 158, 163, 177, 178
excavation, 49, 50, 67
exclusion, 109
execution, 36
experience, 20, 150
expert, 17
expertise, 13–15
exploration, 22, 161
exposure, 126, 135
extract, 8, 89, 95, 99, 100, 102, 106, 147
extraction, 19, 21, 22, 43, 50, 71, 88, 94, 96, 97, 99, 102–105, 107, 147–150, 153, 161, 162

face, 62, 74, 104, 119, 120, 130, 147, 161, 167, 171, 176
facility, 74
family, 78, 79, 112, 128, 176–178

farmer, 146
faucet, 158
feasibility, 63
Fiberglass cisterns, 66
field, 137, 138
filling, 116, 127, 128
filter, 37, 38, 67, 81, 85, 89, 109–112
filtering, 38, 45, 80
filtration, 37, 39, 74, 81–83, 85, 91, 109–112, 119, 137
finish, 66
fish, 22
flood, 51, 169–171, 176
flooding, 168, 169, 171, 174, 176
floor, 74
flotation, 118
flow, 19, 21, 29–35, 37, 39, 42, 45, 48–50, 84, 85, 92, 98, 101, 110, 111, 166, 170
fluid, 98, 105, 110
flushing, 59, 74
fog, 9, 95, 96, 161
following, 1, 3, 5, 11, 14, 16, 17, 19, 23–25, 29, 31, 32, 38, 45, 54, 55, 57, 58, 61, 64, 65, 72, 75, 76, 79, 82, 84, 88, 90, 102, 103, 105, 109, 111, 112, 115, 123–126, 129, 130, 150–154, 159, 160, 162, 164, 165, 167, 168, 172–174, 176, 178
food, 11, 123, 127
foot, 30
force, 92, 98, 105
form, 118
formation, 15, 39–42
formula, 78, 106
foundation, 67, 68, 83, 165
framework, 152, 161, 167

freezing, 21, 74
frequency, 69, 142
freshness, 178
freshwater, 9, 44
frost, 68
function, 45
future, 8, 42, 44, 131, 159, 173, 176

gallon, 128
garage, 74
gender, 1
geology, 14–16, 30, 45
glass, 127
goal, 18, 153, 165
government, 13–15, 30, 176
grade, 123, 127
gradient, 19, 45
gravel, 42, 49, 67, 110
gravitation, 92
gravity, 46, 92–94, 100
ground, 30, 40, 42, 49–51, 67, 89, 92
groundwater, 11, 13–15, 17–19, 29–31, 34, 46, 51, 54, 57, 147, 159, 161, 162, 166
group, 39
growth, 68, 123–126, 146
guidance, 153
guideline, 142, 166
gutter, 74

habitat, 51
hand, 4, 30, 99, 100, 102, 105
handle, 67, 100
harm, 146
harvesting, 8, 10–12, 14, 15, 20, 34–36, 39, 54, 56, 58–62, 65, 75, 77–80, 85, 91, 94–96, 120, 125, 145, 147, 151, 152, 161
health, 2–5, 20, 27, 31, 69, 111, 112, 133, 135–138, 141, 143, 151, 152, 164, 173, 176
heat, 82
heating, 68
height, 88, 98
help, 11, 14, 17, 30, 45, 49, 50, 65, 68, 71, 111, 112, 127, 136, 158, 159, 169, 173
hiker, 38
hole, 30
home, 85, 127, 178
homeowner, 65, 74
host, 133
household, 65, 78, 80, 85, 110, 134, 157, 163, 173
housing, 17
human, 3, 20, 31, 48, 80, 83, 89, 162
humidity, 9, 89, 94
hydration, 3, 22, 24, 25, 34
hydraulic, 19, 49, 50, 97, 105–107
hydrology, 14, 16, 30, 64, 83
hydrostatic, 106
hygiene, 3–5, 22, 166, 171, 173
hyporheic flows, 42

identification, 141
impact, 14, 17, 20, 43, 51, 56, 97, 136, 158, 159, 163, 169, 174
implement, 20, 115, 128, 166, 175
implementation, 22, 57, 86, 91, 120, 165
importance, 3, 5, 15, 65, 126, 153, 159, 166
include, 4, 8, 14, 15, 20, 37, 38, 40, 51–53, 63, 67, 70, 72, 74,

Index 187

75, 77, 84, 88, 95, 99, 103, 118, 119, 123–126, 133–135, 138, 146, 153, 162–164, 166, 168, 170, 177
increase, 21, 49–51, 113
individual, 1, 22, 135, 157
infection, 115
infiltration, 17, 40, 49, 51, 57, 71
influence, 1, 3, 18, 31, 32, 34, 42
information, 13–16, 18, 137
infrastructure, 12, 86, 165, 167, 173, 176
ingenuity, 89
inlet, 67, 68
inspection, 30
install, 66, 68
installation, 76, 112, 166
instance, 10, 11, 20, 21, 47, 96, 146, 160
insulation, 66
intake, 1, 67
integration, 83, 85
intensity, 75
interplay, 42
interpretation, 139
intrusion, 170
inverter, 104
investing, 12
investment, 12, 62
involvement, 159, 167
iodine, 38
irrigation, 17, 50, 59, 61, 65, 74, 154, 157, 158
issue, 20, 68
Ithaca, 61

jurisdiction, 145, 148, 153

knowledge, 10, 14, 15, 17, 30, 31, 42

label, 128
laboratory, 137
lack, 4
land, 21, 29, 30, 34, 40, 54, 56, 147, 168
landowner, 154, 155
landscape, 153
landscaping, 17, 170
law, 92, 153–155
layer, 19, 67
lead, 2, 4, 5, 20–22, 68, 71, 89, 111, 123, 133, 147, 151, 173
leakage, 66
learning, 176
leave, 39
levee, 176
level, 1, 13, 19, 67, 85, 136, 138
life, 10, 22, 137, 176, 179
lifesaver, 11
lifespan, 66, 69, 71
light, 68, 115, 124, 126
limestone, 15, 30, 45
limit, 173
limitation, 111
line, 68
lining, 49
liquid, 95
liter, 74, 85
livestock, 21
living, 112, 159
load, 21
locating, 15, 18, 19, 30, 44, 101
location, 30, 63–65, 98, 100, 151
longevity, 61, 67, 68, 74, 77, 122
loss, 20, 66, 67, 176

maintaining, 3, 12, 34, 35, 62, 122, 126, 128, 141, 143, 171, 179
maintenance, 12, 51, 53, 54, 57, 59, 61, 66, 68–70, 74, 77, 111, 126–128, 141–143
making, 11, 21, 49, 66, 94, 97, 102, 105, 133, 138, 168
management, 4, 5, 12, 14, 15, 18, 22, 39, 42, 44, 54, 56, 83, 86, 128–130, 136, 140, 147, 151, 153, 155, 161, 173, 176
manner, 128
manufacturer, 38
map, 19
Mark, 127, 178
material, 45, 67, 78, 89, 122, 126
matter, 81, 96, 112, 113, 137
mean, 10
means, 51, 79, 123, 127
measure, 136–138, 179
measurement, 34
measuring, 138
medium, 109, 111
membrane, 119, 120, 137
metal, 78, 95, 96, 101
meter, 30, 136, 137
method, 8, 9, 34–36, 46, 75, 77, 80–82, 94, 95, 98, 99, 101, 105, 107, 116–119, 127, 128, 137, 138, 161
Microbubbles, 118
microfiltration, 119
micron, 81
minimum, 166
mitigation, 133, 169, 171
mix, 66
mm, 159

model, 174
moisture, 9, 30, 47, 92, 94–97, 161
monitor, 3, 33, 111, 141
monitoring, 21, 30, 34, 71, 111, 115, 125, 126, 128, 138, 140–143, 158, 159, 166
mortar, 66, 67
movement, 18, 30, 35, 40, 42, 49, 91, 92

Namibia, 96
nanofiltration, 119
nature, 89, 91, 176
need, 5, 12, 29, 30, 65, 73, 78, 79, 100, 123, 148, 167, 174, 177
network, 46
New Orleans, 176
New York, 61
Newton, 92
night, 95, 96
non, 61, 66, 74, 118, 127, 151, 152
number, 165

obligation, 151
odor, 39
one, 12, 30, 37, 42, 45, 66, 68, 97, 98, 100–102, 110, 117, 127, 157, 167
operation, 99–102, 111
opportunity, 36
option, 105
order, 13
osmosis, 111, 119, 161
other, 4, 11, 19, 22, 24, 66–68, 92, 101, 112, 124, 127, 141, 176
outage, 171, 172
outlet, 35, 67

Index

output, 31, 103
ownership, 21
oxygen, 21, 137
ozone, 118

paint, 74
Pakistan, 176
panel, 103, 104
parameter, 139
part, 115
particulate, 81, 96
Pascal, 105
patch, 30
path, 49
peer, 14
people, 163
percolation, 12, 19, 49–54, 57–59
period, 20, 39, 81
permeability, 40, 50
Permeable, 49
permission, 21
person, 78, 157, 162, 165, 166, 173
phase, 175
piston, 100
pit, 67
plan, 161, 162, 164, 169, 178
planning, 17, 19, 34, 36, 79, 86, 91, 94, 128, 164, 167
plant, 91
planting, 50
plastic, 39, 82, 95, 101, 116, 127
plumbing, 85
point, 95
pollution, 10, 20, 137, 162
polyester, 110
pond, 19, 50–53, 57
population, 146, 165, 166
potential, 12, 18, 20, 22, 23, 30, 31, 36, 37, 39, 44, 48, 55, 56, 59, 67, 68, 78, 89, 96, 115, 131, 133, 137, 140, 143, 147, 151, 152, 161, 164, 165, 171, 174
power, 62, 91, 102, 103, 171–173
practicality, 96
practice, 12, 127
precipitation, 40, 59, 75, 159, 160
preparation, 10, 169, 171
preparedness, 29, 164, 169, 174, 179
presence, 11, 15, 21, 30, 42, 112, 113, 137, 138, 160
pressure, 42, 45, 66, 68, 98, 100, 105–107, 110, 111
pricing, 167
principle, 75, 97, 98, 100, 101, 105, 109, 112, 146
priority, 147
process, 20, 57, 66, 79, 83, 85, 102, 109, 116, 118, 143, 147, 149, 150
production, 123
professional, 70
program, 61
project, 17, 68, 74
proof, 147
property, 21, 59, 146, 154, 169, 170, 176
protection, 12, 68
protozoa, 112, 133
proximity, 31, 65, 160
pump, 74, 97, 100, 104, 106
pumping, 97, 99, 104, 105
purification, 22, 36, 38, 91, 96, 109–112, 117, 118, 120, 136, 138, 170
purity, 123
purpose, 136, 137

quality, 8, 13, 15, 18, 21–27, 31, 34–36, 63, 69–71, 74, 83, 85, 96, 102, 109–112, 120, 122, 125–128, 133, 134, 136–138, 140–143, 170
quantity, 21, 63
quest, 20

radiation, 82
radius, 88
rainfall, 8, 10, 11, 20, 21, 29, 34, 50, 51, 54, 75, 78, 80, 159, 168
rainwater, 8, 12, 17, 19, 54, 56, 58–62, 67, 74–85, 125, 160, 161
Rainwater Harvested, 80
range, 2, 115, 153, 168
rate, 29, 31, 34, 40, 45, 49, 90, 92, 110
rating, 112
rationing, 165–167, 173
reaction, 118
readiness, 171
recharge, 17, 49–51, 54, 57, 65
recovery, 173, 175, 176
reduce, 11, 49, 117, 126, 169, 172
reduction, 61, 112
refrigeration, 95
region, 19, 30, 49, 125
regulation, 12
relationship, 165
reliability, 10, 12, 20, 21, 31, 32, 34, 39, 68
reliance, 22, 159
reminder, 127
removal, 49, 90, 110, 118
replenishment, 17
reporting, 166
research, 14, 65, 161

reservoir, 35
resilience, 12, 29, 59, 61, 62, 74, 97, 120, 161, 164, 171, 176
resistance, 49, 122
resource, 3, 15, 22, 36, 39, 48, 65, 77, 83, 86, 120, 123, 126, 128, 153, 159, 164, 179
response, 146, 167, 174–176
result, 22, 126, 140, 147
retention, 19, 49
retrofitting, 72–74
review, 167
right, 18, 65, 68, 120, 122, 146, 147
risk, 21, 68, 71, 117, 123, 124, 126, 168, 176
river, 21, 22, 45, 46, 65, 146
rock, 15, 18, 30, 37, 42, 45, 92, 128
role, 3, 5, 63, 91, 97, 123
roof, 67, 74, 78, 85
rotate, 126–128, 178
rotation, 127, 128
rule, 147
run, 12
runoff, 10, 11, 19–21, 31, 40, 50, 51, 67, 71, 78, 85, 134
rust, 66, 112

s, 1, 3, 8, 17, 30, 35, 38, 39, 45, 61, 74, 80, 89, 92, 98, 102, 105, 136
safety, 20, 21, 24, 25, 31, 66, 80, 96, 102, 112, 115, 122, 123, 126, 128, 136, 138, 140, 141, 143, 170, 173
sand, 42, 81, 110, 111
sandstone, 30, 45
sanitation, 3–5, 22, 34, 166
saturation, 40, 89
saving, 158, 166

Index 191

scarcity, 20, 24, 25, 59, 66, 74, 89, 96, 97, 102, 105, 120, 128, 130, 157, 159, 161, 162, 164, 165, 167, 176
scenario, 19, 30, 104, 128
schedule, 128
screen, 81
seal, 67
sealability, 122
sealant, 67
sealing, 68, 74, 126
season, 34, 65
seawater, 9, 161
section, 3, 7, 13, 15, 22, 25, 31, 34, 37, 39, 44, 48, 51, 57, 59, 63, 66, 69, 72, 75, 77, 80, 89, 92, 99, 109, 112, 120, 123, 126, 133, 141, 145, 147, 151, 153, 157, 159, 161, 165, 176
security, 12, 77, 80
sediment, 21, 48, 49, 85, 109–111, 128
sedimentation, 83
seep, 51
seepage, 8
selection, 51, 54, 66, 123
self, 62, 83
sense, 101
separation, 109
series, 30, 111
set, 20, 67, 138
setting, 74
settling, 67
sewage, 67
shape, 42, 49, 54
share, 30
shingle, 78
significance, 22, 41, 140

siphon, 98, 101
siphoning, 97, 99, 100
site, 51, 52, 54, 63, 65, 67, 138
situation, 126, 133, 176
size, 42, 54, 67, 77, 78, 109, 110, 122
sizing, 77–79
skill, 20, 24, 27, 44
slope, 30
snow, 51, 67, 168
snowmelt, 34
soil, 11, 18, 20, 30, 37, 40, 42, 49–51, 56, 57, 65, 89, 92
solar, 99, 103, 104, 117, 161
solid, 67, 68, 109
solubility, 136
solution, 59, 68, 77, 85, 90, 102, 105, 138
source, 7, 8, 20, 25, 29–31, 33, 34, 44, 59, 65, 71, 83, 98, 101, 104, 128, 145, 146, 154, 161
sourcing, 17, 18, 22, 27
space, 105
spectrum, 115
spout, 100
spread, 4
spring, 29–35, 37–39, 154
springs, 34
stability, 11, 67
stagnation, 68
state, 147, 148, 151
status, 3
steel, 66
step, 15, 17, 20, 29, 39, 51, 52, 63, 67, 72, 75, 83, 112, 138, 148, 150, 174, 175
stewardship, 74
stick, 101
stockpiling, 176–179

storage, 35, 51, 58, 59, 61, 66–68, 72–76, 78–80, 83, 84, 120, 122–130, 147–150, 164, 169, 171, 178
store, 10, 12, 15, 35, 56, 128, 150
strategy, 9, 50, 128, 165, 176
stream, 30, 43, 49
strength, 66
structure, 35, 67, 68, 92
study, 17, 34
subsurface, 42, 46
success, 68, 94, 101
suction, 100
sufficiency, 62, 83
suitability, 31, 74
summary, 12, 65, 83
sun, 102
sunlight, 39, 82, 103, 116, 124
supply, 10–12, 29, 36, 57, 63, 68, 69, 71, 75, 83–86, 91, 97, 107, 112, 115, 125–128, 131, 160, 162, 165, 166, 171, 173, 179
support, 67, 155, 158, 176
surface, 7, 8, 10–13, 19–22, 24–27, 29–31, 34, 39, 42, 44, 46, 47, 51, 56, 71, 75, 78, 103, 111, 118, 159, 166, 178
surrounding, 19, 25, 44, 45, 69, 145, 147
survey, 15, 18, 19, 65
survival, 3, 5, 7, 9–12, 15, 18, 20, 22, 24, 25, 27, 29, 31, 34, 36, 39, 42, 44, 48, 50, 65, 88, 89, 94, 97, 99, 102, 107, 117, 120, 126, 133, 136, 140, 157, 159, 161, 167, 168, 176
survivalist, 19

susceptibility, 135
sustainability, 17, 34, 42, 48, 51, 59, 62, 65, 74, 77, 85, 86, 143, 158, 161
synergy, 89
system, 14, 54, 59–62, 67–69, 71, 72, 74, 75, 77–80, 83, 85, 91, 95, 103–105, 109–112, 125, 128, 147, 167, 173
São Paulo, 167

table, 13, 15, 17, 29, 34, 45, 65
tank, 35, 76, 79, 85
tap, 11, 44, 45, 178
target, 81
taste, 112
technique, 35, 45, 46, 94, 97, 98, 100, 107, 116, 136
technology, 105, 161
temperature, 11, 12, 21, 94, 112, 126, 136
term, 12, 15, 22, 53, 58, 59, 165, 175, 176
terrain, 18
test, 30, 39, 70, 125, 127, 136–140, 142
testing, 21, 39, 127, 128, 136–138, 140–143, 170
Texas, 147
texture, 92
the Atacama Desert, 96, 161
the United States, 146
theory, 34, 37, 89, 112, 165
thermometer, 136
time, 19, 31, 33, 66, 112, 120, 126
toilet, 59, 74
tool, 89, 102
top, 81

topography, 51, 56, 57
total, 166
trace, 137
track, 166
tracking, 178
transpiration, 20
trap, 110
treatment, 21, 80, 83, 85, 111, 119, 125, 126
trip, 39
tsunamis, 173
tube, 88, 98, 101
turbidity, 21, 112, 134, 136, 138
type, 15, 51, 56, 57, 89, 110, 135

ultrafiltration, 119
underground, 10–15, 17, 22, 37, 40–51, 75–77, 85, 91, 92, 94, 97, 99–102, 105, 107, 112, 115, 120, 129, 130, 138, 140, 141, 145, 147, 151, 152, 154, 160, 171
understanding, 3, 5, 12, 15, 16, 18, 20, 24, 27, 31, 34, 36, 41, 42, 44, 48, 50, 56, 65, 74, 77, 80, 89, 91, 94, 97, 107, 115, 130, 140, 143, 150, 152, 155, 159, 167, 171, 173, 176
unit, 31
upstream, 31, 146
urine, 3
usability, 126, 141
usage, 16, 17, 34, 83, 138, 155, 157–159, 166, 167, 172, 173
use, 3, 8, 20, 22, 24, 27, 32, 38, 40, 56, 65, 66, 74, 78, 80, 99, 101, 110–112, 118, 120, 122, 127, 136, 145–147, 177
user, 101, 146
utilization, 129

vacuum, 100
validity, 101
vapor, 95
variability, 20, 161
variation, 29, 34
variety, 48, 81
vegetation, 30, 47, 50, 56, 160, 161
velocity, 98
viability, 14
vicinity, 23
viscosity, 110
visibility, 31
volume, 20, 21, 31, 34, 45, 69, 72, 75

waste, 4, 11, 21, 134, 158
water, 1, 3–5, 7–27, 29–31, 33–51, 54, 56–59, 61–63, 65–69, 71–75, 77–86, 88–107, 109–113, 115–120, 122, 123, 125–131, 133–138, 140–143, 145–155, 157–174, 176–179
waterborne, 117, 133, 141
wavelength, 115
wealth, 16
wear, 127
weather, 11, 67
web, 148
week, 177, 178
weight, 67, 68
well, 3, 5, 19, 27, 45, 48, 57, 63–65, 67, 69–71, 103, 104, 138, 147, 162, 164, 178
wicking, 89

wildlife, 51
Winkler, 137
winter, 21, 74
witching, 101, 102

work, 82
world, 42, 129

year, 69, 78, 127, 142, 158, 162, 178
yield, 16, 55